GOD'S HEART, GOD'S HANDS

GOD'S HEART, GOD'S HANDS

Denise George

new hope
PUBLISHERS

Birmingham, Alabama

New Hope® Publishers
P. O. Box 12065
Birmingham, AL 35202-2065
www.newhopepublishers.com

Dewey Decimal Classification: 248.843
Subject Headings: WOMEN-RELIGIOUS LIFE

God's Heart, God's Hands was originally published by LifeWay Press.

ISBN: 1-56309-831-8

N044118 • 0604 • 5M1

For my sister,
Jill Marie Wyse,
with joy in our newfound
love and friendship!

Contents

Introduction

This book is about real women with real problems. Today's women are hurting. They have been hurt—physically, mentally, emotionally—by life, by others, by circumstances, by tragedies.

Jesus entered human flesh with a purpose. He walked the same long road we walk. Jesus encountered the same real women with the same real problems that we encounter.

With God's heart, Jesus reached out. With God's hands, Jesus changed lives. Women hurt by life's experiences need God's heart and God's hands. They yearn for changed lives.

Christian women who proclaim the lordship of Christ have a purpose. With Christ at the helm of our lives, we can make a difference; we can impact a hurting world. We have much work to do! With Christ in our hearts, we can learn to reach out in the same way He reached out. For we are God's heart and God's hands.

How to Use This Book as a Study

God's Heart, God's Hands is a biblically-based study, written especially for Christian women. The purpose of this study is to show Christian women the vast need for service and to teach some ways to reach out in Christ's love to women who hurt. It is written for women of all evangelical denominations, all ages, and all walks of life. It is designed to be used both as a personal study and tool for individual ministry, and as a group study and tool for group ministry.

While the limited space of a book does not allow us to include all the issues that bring pain to women across the world, *God's Heart, God's Hands* attempts to outline some of the major issues women experience in contemporary society.

Some chapters are longer and more detailed than other chapters. I suggest the participant in this study read one chapter each week. The participant may want to read the entire chapter at one sitting or to read sections of it throughout the week. At the end of the week, join with a small group of women (no more than six or eight) to discuss the contents of the chapter. "Questions for Reflection and Discussion," located at the end of each chapter, are provided to encourage personal reflection as well as group reflection and discussion. You may wish to close the group meeting with the suggested prayer.

I have provided pages for journaling at the end of each chapter. Perhaps as you read each chapter, God will impress upon your heart specific needs in your community. Use these pages to record both the needs and their answers. You can also use these pages to record available resources, such as names of Christian attorneys, crisis intervention agencies, and additional hotlines.

My personal prayer is that *God's Heart, God's Hands* will be a tool through which God can speak to you. May it touch your heart and encourage you to reach out to hurting women in His healing name.

Denise George

A Drink of Water: Reaching Out with God's Truth

Helping Women Through Broken Relationships

Bible Study: Read John 4:4–42

*T*he townswomen of Sychar must have gossiped about her behind her back. Early mornings, while they filled their water jars at the local well, she may have hidden in her house. Then at noon, during the hottest hour of the day, she went out to fill her empty jars. She surely longed to avoid their accusing eyes and unkind looks as they shook their heads in disgust.

She could have been a middle-aged woman with a sad, bitter heart. We can imagine that five husbands had used her and then run off, perhaps with younger and prettier women. She now lived with a man who would possibly do the same thing: use her, promise her everything, and toss her aside.

On a hot afternoon the woman we know only as the Samaritan woman lugged her water jar to Jacob's well. Little did she know that the water she would find would change her life forever. For on this day, she would meet Jesus.

"Will you give me a drink?" (v. 7) Jesus asked when she arrived at the well. He spoke to her not as the other men in town but as a loving father to his cherished daughter. Jesus reached out to her with God's truth. He offered what only He could give her—living water to fill her empty heart. The Savior's love replaced the bitterness in her heart. Jesus gave her a new life brimming with love and purpose.

She drank from Jesus' cup that day—His cup of forgiveness. Jesus forgave her. Grace equipped her to forgive the townspeople who may have used, abused, and despised her. She must have forgiven them completely because she ran back into town to tell them about the saving Messiah and the living water He could give. For they, too, needed to drink from the cup of forgiveness. They, too, had bitter, unforgiving hearts. They, too, had a thirst that only the loving Father could quench.

She may have even forgiven the men who had used her, promised her everything, and tossed her aside. How can our hearts hold bitterness when Christ has so freely given us beautiful new lives and has forgiven and forgotten our sinful pasts?

Life is made up of relationships. Since humans are imperfect, forgiveness plays an essential role in life's journey in relating to others. How can we forgive fully, completely as Christ has forgiven us when we are faced with seemingly unforgivable wrongs against us?

Susan's Story

Susan married Wayne, a successful surgeon, 26 years ago. She dedicated herself to him. She supported and encouraged him through long years of medical school, maintained their home, and became mother to their two children. She loved her role as a Christian wife and mother.

During the first half of their marriage, Wayne and Susan both worked hard to support themselves and to pay Wayne's expensive medical-school tuition. They refinished yard-sale furniture for their tiny, two-room apartment. They ate a lot of inexpensive meals. Shortly after he graduated, Wayne found a good-paying position in an out-of-state hospital. They moved out of their apartment, said goodbye to family and friends, and bought their first house near the hospital. They enrolled their 12-year-old daughter in a nearby elementary school, and their son began kindergarten.

After the long struggle through school, Susan looked forward to a comfortable future with her husband and children.

That's when . . . you guessed it. It's becoming an all too familiar story these days. Wayne met an attractive young nurse at the hospital, divorced Susan, and married the younger woman.

It broke Susan's heart.

Divorce

Divorce means the death of a marriage, the death of a family's future together. We are saddened but no longer shocked when we hear that friends, acquaintances, neighbors, or fellow church members are filing for divorce. It happens so often these days. We hurt for the husband, wife, and for the children caught in the middle of the painful parting.

Consider that:

- Two-thirds of all first marriages probably will end in separation or divorce.
- Seventy-five percent of second marriages fail (*Marriage Savers*).
- One million American children will see their parents divorce this year (*Marriage Savers*).
- Sixteen million children in the United States live with one parent. (The number has almost doubled since 1970.)
- Forty-five percent of female-headed families with children at home live in poverty. But only 8 percent of married couples with children under age 18 live in poverty (*American Demographics*).
- Eighty-one percent of children in single-parent homes live with their mothers.
- If current trends continue, 61 percent of American children will spend some time in a single-parent household before they are 18 years old. Of this group, half will see a second divorce before they turn 18.[1]
- According to the Rockford Institute, if you look at all marriages that took place last year, about 45 to 50 percent will eventually end in divorce. This conclusion is based on the fact that the annual ratio of divorces-to-marriages has been about one in two for more than a generation. There has been a slight downward trend in the past several years, but basically that number has been consistent since no-fault

divorce began in 1970. Among the 55-and-older population, for example, marriages are quite stable. Most marriages that fail do so before the partners reach their mid-40s.

- George Barna, author of *The Future of the American Family*, finds that the divorce rate among born-again Christians (27 percent) and fundamentalist Christians (30 percent) actually is higher than the rate for non-Christians (23 percent). And yes, his survey asked if the people had been divorced before or after they became Christians. Eighty-seven percent said *after.* "A person's faith doesn't seem to have a lot of effect on whether they'll get divorced. Even among born-again Christians, most don't exhibit attitudes or behaviors any different than non-Christians." Those numbers, once publicized, met with only mild surprise. "That's the milieu they live in. Either they've been through a divorce or they know someone who has. It's no longer the shocking reality that it was 30 or 40 years ago."

The Last Thing

Susan thought divorce was the last thing that could ever happen to her. It caught her totally off guard. Like many other women, Susan found herself alone, the sole support for her two children, and hurting financially and emotionally.

"I felt so afraid," Susan said. "I didn't know if I could make it on my own."

Susan also felt intense hatred for Wayne and for his new wife and family. Bitterness and resentment rooted itself in Susan's heart. She moved out of their new home and back into a small apartment. Then she began the long process of pulling her life back together and dealing with her hurt.

Relationships

We were created by God to be in relationship with one another. In too many marriages, harmony in relationship is the exception, not the rule. The closer the relationship with another, the more fertile the breeding ground for conflict. The paradox is that the closer the relationship, the easier it should be to resolve conflict, right wrongs, and overcome hurts. When we are intimate with another person as in a marriage relationship, we are extremely open and vulnerable. We also should know that person like we know no other and practice unconditional love and forgiveness. Unfortunately, the most significant and humiliating pain seems to occur in marriage—the one relationship that should offer the greatest security, happiness, and fulfillment.

The closeness of a marriage partnership, built on mutual trust and love, intensifies the hurt when separation occurs. When the one with whom a woman is most intimate chooses to end the relationship, the woman is most often left confused, devastated, and bitter.

Many women feel they could more easily cope with the death of a spouse than with the pain caused by the loss of a husband through abandonment and/or divorce. In abandonment or divorce, women are not only left hurting by grief and loss, but often suffer a severe blow to their self-esteem. Yet they must continue to deal with their hurt while relating to the ex-spouse in child support, custody, and visitation agreements. In addition, Christians—the ones who should most readily forgive—often turn away, not quite knowing how to show the love and support these women so desperately need.

Divorce and Forgiveness

In marriage, more than in any other relationship, forgiveness is the key. Forgiveness is also the key if the marriage ends in divorce.

Put yourself in Susan's situation for a moment. Could you forgive Wayne if he had been your husband and the father of your children?

Could you forgive Wayne while watching him give Hawaiian vacations, expensive clothes, and a dream house to his new wife while you struggle to keep your son and daughter in shoes that fit?

Could you forgive Wayne knowing that he was loving, providing for, and rearing his new wife's children after deliberately abandoning his own children?

After investing 26 years of your life with Wayne, could you wipe the slate clean knowing that his new wife and children are enjoying financially what you struggled to obtain?

Could you truly let go of the bitterness and resentment and forgive Wayne, knowing that forgiving him would mean forgiving the pain he caused you, blocking from your mind the way he hurt you and the children, continuing to love him, and wishing the best for him with his new family? Could you include him, his new wife, and her children in your daily prayers?

Not sure? Welcome to the human race.

True Forgiveness: Is It Possible?

I believe that it is not *humanly* possible to forgive someone who has deeply and deliberately hurt you and those you love. Forgiveness is a mystery, a process we cannot understand, a gift from God given freely to us.

No doubt, some people will heartily disagree with that statement. The trend of the day is to make everything humanly possible, even forgiveness. As a society, we find it difficult to admit that we can't always "fix" everything—whether a physical, emotional, mental, or spiritual problem—with some sort of device or method.

Contrary to popular opinion, forgiveness is not a three-step, ten-step, or twelve-step program. Forgiveness does not come naturally to us. Our natural tendency is to get even. Revenge, not unlimited pardon, is our common instinct.

If he hits you, punch him back.

If she curses you, curse her.

We do this "natural thing" of seeking revenge person to person, family to family, and nation to nation.

"Turn the other cheek"? Not on your life! Someone must pay. Lawyers in our eye-for-an-eye, tooth-for-a-tooth society are busier than they've ever been.

But God encourages us to take a route opposite the "get even" road. He tells us to forgive and to love. He shows us the other way to life. God's love is stronger than our basic instinct for revenge.

No doubt, you have met women who have been hurt by divorce, abandonment, and rejection. Perhaps you too are among the hurting. Bitterness so often accompanies divorce, abandonment, and rejection that forgiveness seems impossible; but forgiveness is essential for healing the hurt, for draining the bitterness, for beginning life with new purpose. You and I must share with others that, by God's grace, they can forgive. It probably won't happen overnight, but it can happen.

A Friend's Betrayal

Sometimes rejection by a good friend can fill a woman's heart with bitterness. You may have a good friend you believe is honest, supportive, helpful, and genuinely loves you. She has some problems, as we all do, and you give her a 100 percent listening ear whenever she calls on you. You spend hours listening to her, praying for her. When she needs to get away for the weekend with her husband, you keep her children. You invest time, energy, love, and prayer into your relationship with her. You love her like a sister; you trust her enough to confide your heart's secrets; you feel free to share your joy and your pain because you truly believe she rejoices with you and shares sorrows with you. You think she will be your friend for life.

Then one day she turns against you. She rejects you, shuns you, and spreads the secrets of your heart that you've entrusted to her.

Her unexpected rejection, her lack of love, sensitivity, and caring leave you in shock. You wonder whether you will ever trust anyone again. You feel confused and hurt, and she acts as if she doesn't care. You wonder if she ever really cared for you or if she was just selfishly using you. (*A-use-sive* behavior can be as painful as *A-bu-sive* behavior.)

You experience pain, hurt, anger, confusion, and genuine sadness over the loss of the friendship. You grieve. You replay her angry, accusing words in your mind. Your heart and soul bubble with bitterness.

Wouldn't It Be Easier Not to Forgive?

Why should we forgive a person who hurts us, rejects us, and betrays us? I've heard people claim that:

- forgiving makes us better persons
- forgiving makes us feel good inside
- forgiving reduces our stress levels.

Perhaps. Several hundred other, easier things would bring about those results. A 30-minute afternoon nap provides the same benefits.

Why should we forgive a person who hurts us? Because Jesus told us to. If for no other reason, that's why we should forgive each other. Quite elementary when you think about it, isn't it?

Jesus said: "You have heard that it was said, 'You shall love your neighbor and hate your enemy.' But I say to you, love your enemies and pray for those who persecute you" (Matt. 5:43–44 RSV).

Those were radical words to the people of Jesus' day. Those are radical words to the people of our day—radical and humanly impossible. Paul wrote to the Colossians: "If any man have a quarrel against any: even as Christ forgave you, so also do ye" (Col. 3:13 KJV). Jesus tells Peter to forgive his erring brother seventy times seven (see Matt. 18:21–35). In other words, Jesus told Peter and He tells us to keep forgiving endlessly.

If God Can Forgive Us . . .

If God can wipe clean our scribbled slate, then how, as women in Christ, can we live with unforgiving spirits toward our brothers and sisters? Nothing will weigh us down in our Christian walk like unresolved anger, bitterness, and resentment. If we are to continue the marathon of life, we must "lay aside every weight" (Heb. 12:1 KJV).

We need to explain to the hurting women around us that forgiveness does not necessarily involve how we feel toward persons we forgive. We may not want to resume the friendships. We can love persons in Christ and still not especially like them or their individual characteristics and ways of relating. The way we feel has little to do with extending the gift of forgiveness. Thank goodness!

Forgiveness is a decision we make, an act of the will. We decide to forgive and then we ask God, through His forgiveness for us, to enable us to forgive the one who has hurt us. We do not forgive in our own strength. We forgive through God's strength. Without God's grace, true forgiveness is not possible.

"We have the capacity to forgive when we have been deeply hurt because Christ within us is able to release forgiveness toward anyone through us. . . . As we forgive one another, we release ourselves from bitterness."[2]

Releasing the Debt

For two years after Wayne divorced Susan, she was an emotional wreck. "I felt intense anger and suffered from deep depression,"

Susan said. "I remember one morning kneeling by my bed and praying. My clothes were spread out in front of me, but I was so depressed I couldn't get dressed. I kept repeating to myself: 'Susan, all you have to do is just take off your nightgown and put on your shirt and jeans.' I was so drained of emotional energy, I was so depressed, I sat on the floor for 30 minutes trying to perform the simple task of getting dressed."

Susan sought the help of a good Christian counselor and several close Christian friends. She decided to forgive Wayne, to release him from the debt of hurting her.

"When I looked in the mirror, I saw a bitter 45-year-old woman staring back at me," she remembers. "And I told myself: 'Susan, you're a bitter young woman, and one of these days you will be a bitter *old* woman if you don't forgive Wayne and start to heal.' The last thing in the world I wanted to be was a bitter old woman!"

Susan still felt the pain of betrayal and rejection, but she prayed that God would enable her to make the decision to forgive Wayne.

"I couldn't do it on my own," she recalls. "It was God in me that forgave Wayne. I also prayed that God would release me from the bitterness and resentment I felt toward Wayne and his new wife. I couldn't do that on my own either. But I have discovered that God is the God of miracles, and He certainly worked the miracle of forgiveness in my life."

Not long after she forgave Wayne, Susan began to heal. Today she is a happy, vibrant woman who is a joy to be around, a devoted churchwoman who actively reaches out to other women suffering the trauma of divorce. She is a woman with new determination, new purpose.

God's Healing

God provides healing for the injustices and tragedies of life. Nothing or no one can be the source of this healing; it comes only from God. But we can be an agent of God's healing.

Paul wrote, "Be ye kind one to another, tenderhearted, forgiving one another, even as God for Christ's sake hath forgiven you" (Eph. 4:32 KJV).

Does that Scripture also apply to a friend who betrays you? When Cheryl's friend Lela hurt her, she read Paul's words and decided to forgive.

I remember well the day I forgave Lela. I sat in my favorite bedroom chair and remembered her accusing, angry words to me. Then I prayed that God would allow me to forgive her, that He would help me not to hold anything against her, that He would restore the sisterly love I once had for her. I didn't ask Him to restore the friendship. At that point, I just wanted to take the first step. I just wanted to forgive Lela.

I didn't feel much different after I prayed that prayer; but I knew that things were now very different. Through Christ, I had forgiven my friend. I closed my eyes, and in my mind I envisioned the two of us meeting. I heard myself say to her: 'I forgive you, Lela, for hurting me. And I pray that you will also forgive me, for I know I must have also hurt you.' Then I held out my arms and hugged her. Before I opened my eyes, I prayed a simple prayer for the one who had hurt me, asking God to pour out His richest blessings on her and her family.

Since then, whenever I think about her and feel any bitterness, I stop and repeat my prayer for her. I may not always feel as if I've forgiven her, but in my heart and mind I have chosen to forgive her, and I know the process of forgiveness is complete.

Two Misconceptions About Forgiveness

We can have two misconceptions about forgiveness. The first is that if we wait long enough, time will heal our wounds.

Time is usually an enemy, not a friend. Time can increase the hate, bitterness, and resentment that women feel when they decide not to forgive someone who has caused them pain. Hate, then, becomes a way of life, a burden to bear, a way of relating that becomes their very identity. Year after year, some women hold on to their hurts and resentments. Their painful pasts color everything they see, think, and do, every experience they have. Hurts continue to grow, overwhelming them until life becomes a painful moment-by-moment ritual.

Another misconception about forgiveness is that we must understand the whole painful situation or the offender's reasons before we can forgive. We falsely think that we must carefully and painstakingly analyze, scrutinize, digest, and redigest the angry words, the mean attitudes, the cruel actions, and the intended meanings before we can forgive and begin to heal.

But we don't have to understand to accept a painful situation, and we don't have to understand to forgive. Through Christ, we can extend the gift of a second chance and our hearts can be bathed in cleansing forgiveness without understanding all the details of the painful transaction.

A woman may never understand why a person deliberately hurts her. Forgiving another person does not require having to understand. It does not require the other person's asking for forgiveness. Through God's grace, as she has been forgiven by Him, she can choose to forgive another.

A woman can make the decision to forgive and ask God for insight and understanding later. She can allow healing to begin long before she has a clear understanding. By forgiving, she states to God that she accepts His plan for her life, that she aims and strives to become more Christlike in her daily life. She can also trust Christ to take care of the reconciliation, whether on earth or in the completeness of her life with Him. Complete reconciliation is a future happening that God will arrange in His own way.

The Forgiving Spirit

What happens when a Christian woman chooses to live with an unforgiving spirit?

Forgiveness is putting into practice what we believe about God's love and grace. God's Word becomes more real to us when we use it within the daily context of our lives. Only because of God's unconditional love for us can we accept and forgive others with a love unconditional to, and in spite of, their injuries to us.

This type of rare, unconditional love comes only from God and covers a multitude of evils heaped upon us by others. It covers rejecting spouses, betraying friends, and abusive parents. It covers gossiping townspeople who give unkind looks and shake their heads in disgust. It covers those who promise everything and then walk away.

Already Forgiven

Several years ago, in anger I said some unkind words to my husband, Timothy. Later that evening, I walked into Timothy's study, put my arms around his neck, and whispered something like, "I'm sorry, Timothy. Will you forgive me?"

He looked at me and smiled warmly. "It's OK, Denise. Anyway," he said, "I've *already* forgiven you."

Surely, "confession and forgiveness are the concrete forms in which we sinful people love one another."[3]

That's the way I believe Jesus wants us to live and love and forgive each other when He teaches us to pray: "Forgive us our debts, as we also have forgiven our debtors" (Matt. 6:12 RSV).

To a person who lives in Christ's forgiving spirit, forgiveness becomes a way of life. Surely, this is the life God calls us to live.

Could it be that when we kneel in prayer and ask God's forgiveness through Christ for our many wrong choices and evil deeds, He looks at us, smiles warmly, and says: "I've *already* forgiven you"?

Some names have been changed to protect the privacy of those involved.

[1]*American Demographics Desk Reference*, July 1992 (Ithaca, NY: Dow Jones and Company, Inc.), 14–15.
[2]Charles Stanley, *Forgiveness* (Nashville: Thomas Nelson, Inc., 1987), 168–169.
[3]Henri J. M. Nouwen, *In the Name of Jesus: Reflections on Christian Leadership* (New York: The Crossroad Publishing Co., 1989), 46.

Questions for Reflection and Discussion

1. Reread John 4:4–42. Consult a Bible dictionary for help with the following questions:
   • Why did Jesus travel through Sychar?
   • Why was it unusual for a woman to come to Jacob's well at noon instead of morning?
   • What social rules did Jesus break by speaking to a woman? A Samaritan woman? A woman with a bad reputation?
   • Why did Jews not associate with Samaritans?
   • What did Jesus mean by this statement: "Whoever drinks the water I give him will never thirst"? (v. 13)
   • Jesus knew the woman had no husband. Why would He tell her to "Go, call your husband and come back"? (v. 16)
   • Who did the woman first think Jesus was? (See v. 19.)

- Why do you think Jesus so plainly revealed Himself as the Messiah to the woman? (v. 26)
- What did the woman do immediately after receiving God's truth? Did the Samaritan townspeople believe her? Why do you think Jesus chose the Samaritan woman to take the good news into the town of Samaria?

2. How would you define *forgiveness?*

3. What does Jesus Christ say about forgiveness? Why should we forgive others?

4. Do you believe it is humanly possible to forgive those who have deeply hurt you or someone you love? Why or why not?

5. Can you think of any situation in which you feel you could not forgive another? How does Christ make the difference in the situation? Could you forgive that person in Christ? Do you think reconciliation is necessary for forgiveness to be complete?

6. How can you best approach a woman hurt by divorce? How can you help her? What can you do in practical ways? How can you minister to her children? How can you help her to begin to forgive in Christlike love?

7. If you have experienced divorce, what are some ways others reached out to you? How can your experience enable you and others in your group to better help others through divorce, abandonment, and rejection?

8. Do you believe that "harmony in relationship is the exception, not the rule"? Why or why not? Have you seen this to be true in the lives of other women? Ponder and explain.

9. Investigate ways your church can help women and children hurt by the effects of divorce/abandonment. Investigate how many women in your church are hurting in this area. Ask a Christian counselor for help in starting a divorce recovery workshop in your church. You might also consider forming a support group for women hurt by divorce.

10. Find out about community support groups for divorced women and children. Make community support group phone numbers available to church staff, especially those who work in the area of women's ministry.

Prayer

To close your personal devotional time or your group time, you may want to use the following prayer:

Father, teach us how to reach out to hurting women with Your truth. Let us direct them to Jesus, who can offer them Living Water so that they will never thirst again.

We pray for all those women hurt by divorce and abandonment. How it hurts to be rejected by someone we love! Show us how we can show them the importance of forgiveness. We pray that You will be near her as she struggles to forgive those who have hurt her and her children. We pray that she may find a close walk with You, and that You will heal her and give her new purpose.

In Jesus' name, we pray. Amen.

Chapter 1: A Drink of Water

Dropping the Stone: Reaching Out with Forgiveness

Helping Women Forgive Themselves

Bible Study: Read John 8:1–11

S he was guilty of sin. Caught in the act of adultery, the law condemned her to death by stoning. With rocks clenched in their fists, the zealous religious leaders waited impatiently as they tested Jesus. Would Jesus obey Israel's covenant law? Or would Jesus show the sinful woman mercy? Jesus stood there, trapped between His allegiance to the law and His merciful love for those who violated the law.

You probably know the rest of the story. Each man dropped his stone, one by one. Each man knew that he, too, had broken the law of Moses. He knew that he had a sinful heart and that he deserved the sentence of death.

What about the woman we know only as the "adulteress"? She walked away untouched by the rocks of punishment. Jesus forgave her. He set her free.

Did she ever forgive herself?

Jesus had forgiven her and set her free from her sins. She no longer had to carry the heavy burden of her past. Jesus now carried it for her. He freed her from her burden.

Jesus continues to free women from the burden of sin, yet many of them will not forgive themselves. They continue to condemn themselves and cause themselves pain. Often the same women will reach out in forgiveness to those who have hurt them deeply, yet keep the pain fresh in their hearts because they fail to release themselves from their debt.

How Can We Forgive Ourselves

Our failure to forgive ourselves can be devastating. Day after day, it consumes body, mind, and emotions. Slowly it destroys. Our churches and communities are filled with women who are hurt by their misunderstanding of Scripture and their misunderstanding of God's redeeming love. They are the women God has forgiven, and who have forgiven those who have hurt them—but they cannot forgive themselves. How desperately they need to hear the message!

If they have accepted God's forgiveness, if they have made the decision to forgive others, then they must also learn to forgive themselves completely. Otherwise, they cannot find healing; they cannot be completely whole in Christ.

A forgiven, forgiving, cleansed heart is the only kind of heart God can use in His service. A heart filled with bitterness, resentment, and hatred toward God, others, or oneself is a heart with little room for love.

Before we approach these women, however, let us examine our own hearts. How can we reach out to one who has stumbled and fallen if we have heavy, unforgiving hearts ourselves?

Jesus Christ died on the cross to reconcile us to God. We call it atonement, for in His death we find "at-one-ment" with God. We are made right with God.

Jesus Christ is the source of forgiveness. We often accept His forgiveness and forgive those who have wronged us but we fail to forgive ourselves.

We must learn to forgive ourselves. If we choose not to forgive ourselves, we will live a life of sadness, our usefulness to God and to others needlessly sacrificed. We will live a life void of purpose.

In Jeremiah 31:34 God promised to forgive our sins and

remember them no more. In our finite minds we wonder how a God so powerful, so all-knowing, could forget anything. God knows the number of hairs on our heads and He knows our thoughts before we think them. God knows everything we have done and ever will do.

How could God forget? God, in His infinite wisdom, chooses to forget. God makes a choice that what we have done will have no effect on the way He responds in mercy.

Christ died for the forgiveness of our sins—past, present, and future. Nothing we have done is beyond the reach of God's love and power to forgive.

Just ask Iris Blue.

The Prodigal Daughter

Iris Blue's problems began about the time she was born. She can laugh about those early years now.

"I had a problem," she jokes. "I was born big! I was so big that, in elementary school, the teachers would raise their hands and ask me for permission to go to the bathroom! When I started to like boys, I would lean up against the locker and try to look sexy, and the locker would cave in!"

In a more serious tone, Iris reflects: "I really liked boys, and I wanted them to notice me."

But Iris had seen the kind of girls that got the boys' attention, the tall, skinny, beautiful women that adorned billboards and beauty pageant stages. She knew she could never fit into those size 5 Cinderella shoes.

"At an early, early age," Iris recalls, "I had a dream. I wanted to be a lady. I wanted to be gracious and kind, a wife and mother with a family and home. I just wanted to be a lady."

One day Iris asked her mother why she was so big. Her mother told her that God did that to her. That upset Iris. She felt like God had started making a football player and then changed His mind. "And then I found out that the football players' 'shoulders' came off at night. Mine didn't."

Iris was rebellious. When she was a young girl, she ran away from home. Within weeks of the first time she ran away, she got involved in drugs. Within days after that, she was involved in things she never dreamed she'd be involved in—bars, topless clubs.

"I ended up in bad shape," she remembers. "I was strung out on heroin, and I started stealing every day. When I got caught, my mother and dad would cry, and I'd make big promises to change." Iris wanted to keep her promises, but didn't.

By age 17, Iris had been arrested several times, the last time for armed robbery. She remained in jail nine months before being sentenced to eight years in prison. During those years, Iris stayed in constant trouble, and in and out of the hospital trying to kick her drug habit. Due to her arrogant, rebellious behavior, she spent most of her prison time in solitary confinement.

"I cussed, swore, and hit the prison matrons. I ended up being locked in the basement of the prison."

In the dark prison basement, Iris began to think about her life. "My past was so full of guilt I couldn't handle it. I didn't want to think of my present condition. And I sure couldn't think about the future because anybody with any sense knew I'd be an uneducated, ex-convict with a smart mouth. I knew I wouldn't have much chance even if I got out of prison.

"In the privacy of that cell where nobody could see me, I fantasized my life away. I used to pretend I was a lady, pretty and feminine."

When Iris was released from prison, she had not changed. She was still bitter and angry. Before long, she was back on drugs, back in the bars, and running a topless nightclub.

Then came her turning point.

A young Christian man came into the nightclub one night to share his newfound faith. He told Iris that Jesus loved her. But she wasn't interested. He called, visited, and continued to witness to her, but she didn't listen. Finally, he was advised by a minister friend to leave her alone. His friend feared that Iris might influence the young Christian man with her evil ways.

When he told Iris he wouldn't be coming back, she finally listened to him. "I can't be around an old tramp like you anymore!" he blurted out. Then he added: "You don't even know that Jesus Christ could make you a lady!"

Iris will never forget how she felt when she heard his sharp words. "My heart just ripped apart. I had gone down a long road looking in a lot of directions. But that's all I had ever really wanted—just to be a lady.

"Jesus could do that, he told me. He could take an old tramp like me and make her a lady."

Iris felt her heart soften. "I told him: 'I want that. Whatever it takes, I'm ready.'"

Together they went outside, away from the blaring music and flashing lights, away from the dancers in the windows. "I knelt down by the car out front," Iris remembers. "I knelt down and I prayed."

That night, God worked a miracle in Iris Blue's life when she knelt down, confessed her sins, and asked Christ to come into her heart and forgive her. She gave complete control of her life to Jesus Christ, and Christ changed her. He changed her heart, her attitude, her life.

Through His gift of forgiveness, Christ gave Iris a new life, cleansed and pure. He gave her purpose, a new beginning, a second chance.

He made her His daughter. And through the power of the Holy Spirit, He helped her to forgive herself of her depraved past. "That night," Iris Blue remembers, "I knelt down a tramp, but I stood up a lady."

When We Fail

If Christ can forgive us of our many sins, why do we find it so difficult to forgive ourselves? It is often much easier to forgive others who wrong us than it is to forgive ourselves when we make a mistake or fail.

Paul said, "There is therefore now no condemnation for those who are in Christ Jesus" (Rom. 8:1). No Christian needs to experience guilt.

The apostle Paul knew about guilt. Before his unforgettable experience on the road to Damascus, Paul was named Saul. He was a religious fanatic trying his best to stomp out Christianity single-handedly. He went about his task with enthusiasm and fervor; that is, until his blinding encounter with Jesus Christ.

Christ changed Saul's heart. Saul, turned Paul, became one of the greatest missionaries the world has ever known.

Paul accepted Christ's forgiveness, but could Paul ever forgive himself for the havoc and horror he had caused Christ's followers?

Yes, Paul did forgive himself. When he stood before the council and the high priest Ananias, he could say with all honesty: "Brethren, I have lived before God in all good conscience up to this day" (Acts 23:1 RSV).

Paul was able to forgive himself completely for his past. He stood before the Lord and the Sanhedrin with a clear conscience. Therefore, God could use Paul in His work, in His ministry.

What about the Old Testament's King David? He stole another man's wife, who, incidentally, became pregnant from the encounter. Then he had her husband, Uriah, killed on the battlefield. Yet listen to David's prayer for healing and moral restoration in Psalm 51:

> Have mercy on me, O God, according to thy steadfast love; according to thy abundant mercy blot out my transgressions. Wash me thoroughly from my iniquity, and cleanse me from my sin! For I know my transgressions, and my sin is ever before me. Purge me with hyssop, and I shall be clean; wash me, and I shall be whiter than snow. Fill me with joy and gladness. . . . Create in me a clean heart, O God, and put a new and right spirit within me. . . . Restore to me the joy of thy salvation. . . . Deliver me from bloodguiltiness, O God, . . . and my tongue will sing aloud of thy deliverance. . . . A broken and contrite heart, O God, thou wilt not despise (Psalm 51:1–3,7,8,10,12, 14,17 RSV).

Even after all he had done, David could talk of "cleansing," "a clean heart," a "new and right spirit," "deliverance," and of being once again filled with "joy and gladness." Only after he had been forgiven by God, and only after God had enabled him to forgive himself, could King David ask God: "Restore to me the joy of thy salvation" (v. 12). Later, a completely forgiven David, with clear conscience, could write:

> My whole being, praise the Lord. . . . The Lord forgives me for all my sins. . . . He loads me with love and mercy. He satisfies me with good things. He makes me young again, like the eagle. . . . As high as the sky is above the earth, so great is his love for those who respect him. He has taken our sins away from us as far as the east is from west. . . . He knows how we were made. He remembers that we are dust (Psalm 103:1,3–5,11,12,14 NCV).

God's Forgiveness

God's incredible love covers a multitude of sins. We confess. He forgives. In fact, He forgives before we confess.

Charles Stanley writes: "Forgiveness is based on the atoning work of the Cross, and not on anything we do. God's forgiveness does not depend on our confession, nor does His fellowship.

"Confession is a means for releasing us from the tension and bondage of a guilty conscience. When we pray, 'God, You are right. I've sinned against You. I am guilty of this act. I am guilty of that thought,' we achieve release."[1]

Even before we confess our wrongs, God encircles us with His never-ending circle of forgiveness, east becoming west and west becoming east.

We must tell a hurting woman this: If you are a follower of Jesus Christ and have committed your life to Him, you can know without a doubt that God has forgiven your past, present, and future wrongdoings. If you still, however, are struggling under the weight of a heavy load of guilt, know that you are carrying a burden that you need not carry.

Unfortunately, some Christian women carry a burden of guilt for a lifetime. They are wounded by self-induced sores of guilt that never heal. The sores cause them unceasing distress and pain. Sometimes they cover up their sores with busyness, interesting conversation, or the latest television mini-series. But in the dark quiet of the night, in the still early moments of the morning, and during the times in their day when they pause to rest, they are once again aware of their wounds.

We all sin. We all make mistakes, even the most dedicated Christian women; but that doesn't mean we are failures. And that doesn't mean we must be stopped by our failures, never again to be used by God. Christ extends to us His hand of forgiveness, and He offers us the power and the gift of forgiving ourselves when we stumble and fall.

Forgiven and Fit for Ministry

Having a purpose. Being used by God. That's what our Christian lives are all about, isn't it?

Today Iris Blue radiates Christ's love in her presence, her lifestyle, and her speech. She is happily married to a dedicated

Christian man, Duane, and together they have a son, Denim. Iris and Duane travel in full-time ministry, speaking to churches, schools, and prisons, telling everyone what Jesus Christ has done for them and what He can do for all.

In many ways, the story of Iris Blue reminds me of the woman caught in adultery. This woman had a real problem. According to the law of Moses, if two eyewitnesses saw a woman in the act of adultery, the respectable people of the town could pick up rocks and stone her.

So the religious leaders tested Jesus. "What do you think, Jesus?" they asked. "Are we going to obey the law of Moses and kill her?"

Jesus didn't speak. Instead, He slowly knelt and wrote words on the ground. Mystery words.

Then He stood up and said to them: "Let him who is without sin among you be the first to throw a stone at her."

One by one, stones were dropped from sinful hands. Soon Jesus was left alone with the woman before Him.

Ken Gire paints a word picture in his book, *Intimate Moments with the Savior:*

> They are alone now—lawbreaker and lawgiver. And the only one qualified to condemn her, doesn't.
>
> She takes a deep breath. Her heart is a fluttering moth held captive in his hands.
>
> The Savior has stood up for this unknown woman and fought for her. . . . He stands up again, this time to free her.
>
> "Has no one condemned you?" he asks.
>
> Timid words stumble from her lips, "No one, sir."
>
> What comes are words of grace, "Neither do I condemn you . . . ."
>
> . . . She looks into his face. His forehead relaxes. It has been an ordeal for him, too. He takes a breath and his smile seems to say "Go, you're free now."[2]

The Message

This story sends a strong message: Don't judge others. Don't be eager to stand smugly pharisaic and bring to light another's faults and weaknesses. After all, as Scripture tells us, it's difficult to pick out a splinter in your sister's eye when you're carrying a load of firewood in your own eye!

But there is another message in the story, too. Here is a woman who has been dragged through the dirt, proclaimed guilty by the local townspeople, and permanently branded as an adulteress. She thought she would be lying in the street by now, bleeding, dying. Instead, she has been given a new life, a second chance, a new beginning by the one called Jesus.

No doubt, she was forever shunned by the more "decent" townswomen and ridiculed and mocked by the temple leaders. She must have heard the laughter and whispers about her when she carried her water jars to the local well. She must have seen the city's "proper" women divert their eyes when she met them in the marketplace.

But after her encounter with Jesus, she was a daughter of the King! A forgiven daughter of the forgiving King. She had been cleansed, restored, and made whole by the King Himself. In God's eyes her careless, sinful act of adultery had been undone.

The woman was free from sin and guilt. And even with her depraved past, God, no doubt, had future plans for her in His divine work.

God's Promise

God makes us a promise: "If we walk in the light as He Himself is in the light, we have fellowship with one another, and the blood of Jesus His Son cleanses us from all sin. . . . If we confess our sins, He is faithful and righteous to forgive us our sins and to cleanse us from all unrighteousness" (1 John 1:7,9 NASB).

How sad it would be if the woman had gone back to her home and for the remainder of her years had beaten herself down emotionally and mentally for the wrongs that Jesus had forgiven and forgotten. How sad if the woman had become a woman whose past sins, now forgiven, still made her feel dirty, unclean. What a waste of a life.

When we are forgiven, we are no longer guilty. How unfortunate if we allow guilt to cripple us for a lifetime, a lifetime that could be used serving God with joy, gladness, and purpose.

Perhaps guilt is one of Satan's most potent tools.

"Develop a godly tenacity and keep following Christ. You may make mistakes, you may encounter others' disapproval, . . . you occasionally may dishonor the Lord, but realize that you are deeply loved, completely forgiven, fully pleasing, totally accepted, and absolutely complete because Christ died for you and was raised from the dead to give you new life."[3]

What Happened to the Woman?

We will never know what happened to the one we've come to know only as "the adulterous woman." Perhaps in her old age, long after Jesus' death and resurrection, she took her daughters and her granddaughters to the place where, long ago, she had been condemned to die.

Although Scripture doesn't record it, let us try to imagine the possible scene.

"This is where the townspeople dragged me," she points her finger toward the town's main meeting square.

"And this is where Jesus stooped down and wrote on the ground," she tells them.

I can envision her daughters and granddaughters kneeling together, searching for a remnant trace of a letter written by Jesus' own hand.

"And this is where they threw me down, the place where I was to be stoned to death. But Jesus was standing there," she says softly and smiles as she remembers His kind face, His tender eyes. "And He took me by the hand, forgave me, and gave me a new life. A wonderful new life."

"This is where I looked into my Savior's eyes, the place where He cleansed me and made me pure. And this is the place, right here, the very spot, where I was forgiven, where I stood up a lady."

The story of Iris Blue is used by permission.
[1]Charles Stanley, *Forgiveness* (Nashville: Oliver Nelson, 1987), 136.
[2]Ken Gire, *Intimate Moments with the Savior* (Grand Rapids: Zondervan Publishing House, 1989), 57–58.
[3]Gire, 57–58.

Questions for Reflection and Discussion

1. Read Exodus 20:14, Leviticus 20:10, and Deuteronomy 17:5–6 concerning Israel's covenant law that prohibited adultery. What does the law say about punishment for the adulterous woman? Why did the adulterous man not also face punishment?

2. Think about and discuss this statement: "Jesus Christ died on the cross to reconcile us to God. We call it atonement, for in His death, we find 'at-one-ment' with God. We are made right with God."
   What does this statement mean to you?

3. Consider Acts 23:1. How does this verse relate to Paul's later statement in Romans 8:1: "There is therefore now no condemnation for those who are in Christ Jesus"? How has Paul reacted to the forgiveness offered to him through Christ?

4. Read Psalm 51 and Psalm 103. What statements in these verses show David's acceptance of God's forgiveness?

5. Do you believe this statement is true: "A forgiven, forgiving, and cleansed heart is the only kind of heart God can use in His service"? If so, why? If not, why not?
   How does a heart filled with self-imposed guilt keep us from doing God's service and ministry?

6. Do you believe that God has totally forgiven you of your sins? If so, why? How do you relate to the statement in Jeremiah 31:34 about God's remembering our sins no more? How is forgiving and forgetting possible in our lives as we relate to others?

7. If a dictionary is available, find the definition of *guilt*. When is guilt constructive and appropriate? How does the Holy Spirit use guilt in our lives? When is guilt inappropriate? Why is this inappropriate guilt said to be one of Satan's most potent tools? How does he use guilt against us?

8. Read and discuss the following statement:

"Develop a godly tenacity and keep following Christ. You may make mistakes, you may encounter others' disapproval, . . . you occasionally may dishonor the Lord, but realize that you are deeply loved, completely forgiven, fully pleasing, totally accepted, and absolutely complete because Christ died for you and was raised from the dead to give you new life."[4]

What does it mean to be "deeply loved," "completely forgiven," "fully pleasing," "totally accepted," and "complete"?

9. How can you and I approach women who are not able to forgive themselves? How can we help them to forgive themselves and go on with their lives?

What can the church do? What can our community do?

Why is this problem more difficult to deal with than other problems, such as spouse abuse, child abuse, and grief?

What harm comes to a woman who lives with a lifetime of self-imposed guilt?

Prayer

To close your personal devotional time or your group time, you may want to use the following prayer:

> *Father, please forgive us. Help us to forgive others. And help us to forgive ourselves. Show us how to reach out in forgiveness to hurting women in this world. Allow us to share Your Words from Scripture. Allow us to show women, who hurt from their own unforgiven guilt, how to give the load to the Lord and allow Him to deal with it for them. In Jesus' name. Amen.*

Chapter 2: Dropping the Stone

Lonely Beaches, Broken Hearts: Reaching Out with Prayer

Helping Women Cope with Loneliness

Bible Study: Read John 11:1–44

Jesus loved Mary, Martha, and Lazarus. When Lazarus became gravely ill, his sisters summoned Jesus to their side. But before Jesus arrived in Bethany, Lazarus had been dead and buried for four days.

In love and tenderness, Jesus reached out to the bereaved sisters. To Martha, He gave the good news of resurrection. She needed to hear that Jesus is the "resurrection and the life" (v. 25). To Mary, He gave tenderness and joined her in mourning Lazarus' death. Jesus wept with her. And to Lazarus, Jesus reached out with a prayer powerful enough to raise the dead.

"Jesus looked up and said, 'Father, I thank you that you have heard me' " (v. 41).

After His prayer, Jesus turned toward the tomb.

"Lazarus, come out!" Jesus shouted to the man.

Lazarus looked like a mummy as he walked out from the tomb,

still wrapped in funeral clothes from head to toe. But Lazarus was very much alive.

Have you noticed that whenever the situation seemed hopeless, Jesus reached out with prayer? When 5,000 people were desperately hungry, Jesus held five loaves of bread and two fish, and looked toward heaven.

Mark wrote: "He gave thanks and broke the loaves" (Mark 6:41).

When Jesus anticipated His own death, He brought His disciples together in a room to eat their last supper with Him. Jesus took the bread and wine and then prayed. He reached out to His disciples with the comfort of prayer (Mark 14:22–23). He knew they would need it during the next few days.

Scripture records one of Jesus' prayers in John 17. Jesus prayed not only for His disciples, who would face the greatest heartbreak of their lives, but for you and me. He reached out to comfort us with an eternal prayer.

"I pray also for those who will believe in me through their message, that all of them may be one, Father, just as you are in me and I am in you" (vv. 20, 21).

Prayer: A Priority

Jesus made prayer and fellowship with the Father the priority in His life. Whether Jesus reached out to heal a man born blind, lifted small children up onto His lap, or took a whip to the temple money changers, He knew that God was only a heart's whisper away. The Father and Son had unbroken communion throughout the days of Jesus' life on earth. Jesus kept His heart focused on His Father while He worked, traveled, and ministered.

It is no wonder that Jesus reached out with prayer to those who hurt. Prayer was a priority in His life. He lived it, breathed it, and shared it.

You and I can reach out to hurting women with prayer. We can share with them the promise that God is only a heart's whisper away. The Father yearns for each of us to pray and seek His presence. God reaches out to His children with the gift of prayerful fellowship. Yet some Christian women live in despair and loneliness when God's fellowship lies within reach. You and I can tell hurting women today about the gift of prayer, the beauty of fellowship with the Father who loves them more than they will ever know.

Mary

One of the loneliest women I've ever met was Mary. I first met Mary on the beach. Awaiting the sunrise, I had walked miles that morning along the white sands of Gulf Shores, Alabama.

Like the first hints of sunlight suddenly piercing the dark sky, Mary seemed to appear from nowhere. A woman entering her autumn years, she brushed aside strands of hair from her softly lined face. Except for the movement of her hand, she stood very still. As if reminiscing, she focused her eyes on the distant horizon.

Alone on the beach, too early for vacationing crowds, our paths crossed, I believe by divine providence, and we stopped to exchange a greeting.

"A beautiful day," I spoke softly against the backdrop of the docile, rolling whitecaps. "The sea is so calm and blue this morning."

"Yes," the stranger responded. "The water is resting and at peace now." She hesitated and bit her bottom lip lightly. "But sometimes," she continued, her eyes still searching the horizon, "the sea can be sad and gray."

I felt an inner tug at my heart. Mary wasn't talking about the sea at all. Mary was talking about herself.

Sensing a moment of openness and opportunity, I asked a question of the woman whose name I did not yet know. "You seem to be troubled. Can I help you?"

During the next few minutes, I felt God's presence move closer, filling our mouths, minds, and hearts with words usually reserved for longtime friends.

"I come every year now," she said and rubbed her eye with the back of her hand. "I've come every year for 10 years since my beloved husband died. We used to come here together to celebrate our wedding anniversary. I come now to celebrate and to remember our anniversary . . . alone."

We smiled, exchanged first names, and Mary and I talked a while longer. I've forgotten much of what she told me, but I'll never forget her last words.

"Do you know what I miss most since my husband's death? I miss not being number one with anybody. No one loves me like he loved me. I miss him so much."

Then her voice softened and her next words touched my soul. "My heart is broken," she whispered.

I felt a prayer for her form within my heart. I took her hand in mine, and I felt my own eyes mist.

"Mary," I responded, "You're number one with God. God loves you more than anyone ever has or ever could love you. And if you'll let Him, God will heal your broken heart."

For a long moment, Mary dropped her eyes. And all at once, I understood. Mary believed in God. She knew God loved her. She had just forgotten how very much God loved her! In fact, I sensed that at one time in her life, Mary had experienced an intimate and active fellowship with the Father. Perhaps with the unexpected death of her husband, Mary somehow had lost heart and the deep restful and abiding fellowship with the Father.

I believe Mary knew I understood. She smiled at me and squeezed my hand.

She turned her face to the blue sea and, as if pondering again its age-old mysteries, she turned to leave. But before she left, she looked up at me, and with smiling eyes said a simple "thanks."

I stood there silently and watched Mary walk slowly along the shoreline until I could no longer see her. I knew I probably would never see Mary again.

At that moment, I longed to sit down somewhere quiet to talk and pray with her. I wanted to tell her that, at times, I had lost hope. That I, too, had spent long years struggling with difficult questions of faith. That I, too, had once moved far away from the resting place the Lord had created for me in Him. But I had found my way home again, back to the One who loves me most and who waited for me to return.

We have the good news for the Marys we encounter that their hearts will heal if they will allow God to intervene. We can tell them that God loves them, that God made them for Himself, to rest in His love and fellowship. How desperately they need to hear how He came to us in our brokenheartedness; how He often felt His own heart break; how He cried with another Mary who suffered a loved one's loss. We can tell them that the Lord loves them and waits for them to come home, too.

The prayer from my heart reached out to Mary that morning. The Lord "heals the brokenhearted and binds up their wounds" (Psalm 147:3). All the way home that morning, with every cresting wave, I heard the psalmist's promise whisper to me afresh. And all the way home I prayed that Mary could hear it, too.

Loneliness

Loneliness among women is an area of ministry where you and I desperately need to reach out. Lonely women surround us, yearning for someone to care. Christian women also fall victim to loneliness. Why? Some Christian women have forgotten how to pray. They have forgotten just how much the Father loves us, reaches out to us, and yearns for us to pray and seek His presence.

No doubt, you know a woman who is suffering from loneliness. Loneliness is a painful condition. Some women just seem more prone to loneliness than others. Women can feel lonely without good reason. Loneliness can be caused by many factors. Often our most lonely times come when a loved one dies, when we must depart from precious friends, or when we have endured a cross-country/cross-world move. A woman's heart can be wounded by loss and loneliness. Women who have lost a spouse, child, or close friend keenly feel loneliness and loss.

With each fresh sting of loneliness, we can discover anew that the Lord is the Healer of broken hearts. God suffers with us. The Holy Spirit softly whispers to our hearts the lessons of faith we need to learn, and He does so gently and with great love. Perhaps loneliness is the very language of prayer. The Lord hears our lonely cries, binds up our wounds, and promises us a lifetime of tender healing care.

In our most intense pain, the secret of healing is intimate fellowship with Christ.

"Take heart!" Jesus tells us in John 16:33. "I have told you these things, so that in me you may have peace. In this world you will have trouble. But take heart! I have overcome the world."

Christ stands close to us when we hurt; if we stand close to Him, we will discover that we can trust Him, lean on Him, and allow our hurting hearts to bring us closer to Him. Christ offers us His eternal love and strength. How often great lessons of faith and rapid spiritual growth take place when we are in pain and look up to our Creator, our Life-giver.

Going Our Separate Ways

Some called us The Three Musketeers—Helen, Terry, and me. Three women who had little in common except that we all loved God, and we all loved to write about Him.

Terry was the attractive one in her middle thirties, tall, slender, and blonde. She was the well-organized, sharply dressed jet-setter, the mother of a toddler daughter.

I was the one trying to balance a baby on each hip with strained spinach on my sweater. Early thirties, always hurried, never on time, completely unorganized, I was the opposite of Terry.

At 70, Helen was the wise one. Punctual, organized, always laughing, successful in her career, retired. Helen had been blind from birth, but that didn't slow her down at all.

Only the Lord could have ever put the three of us together! We were some trio! We knew each other, warts and all, and we loved each other anyway.

Faithful friends. Doesn't every human heart yearn for that?

We prayed for each other and supported each other during sicknesses, surgeries, worries, and deaths of loved ones. We laughed together. We cried together. We congratulated each other when articles were sold. We encouraged each other when rejection slips for our writing came.

Hardly a day passed that we didn't talk together. We came to love each other dearly and to depend on each other's prayer, advice, and support.

I knew better, but for some reason, I thought the three of us would be together forever.

A decade into our friendship, Helen became very ill with terminal lung cancer. Inoperable. A few months before Helen died, my husband, Timothy, accepted a new position in Birmingham, Alabama, and we moved. Not long after, Terry and her family moved to Denver, Colorado.

I learned again something I knew already about loss and loneliness: it hurts. It hurts a lot.

I also learned something else about loneliness. While I had other friends, and while I was making new friends, the company of other people didn't seem to help heal the grief and emptiness I felt. I desperately missed the tears, laughter, and encouragement of Terry and Helen. I found that I wanted to take long periods of time simply to withdraw into the presence of the Lord. I felt such an urgency to be with Him.

"Paradoxical as it may seem," writes Myron S. Augsburger, "the true cure for loneliness is to get alone with God, to allow one's self to rest in him. Loneliness is corrected by a sense of belonging to God."[1]

I have discovered that intimate fellowship with God is the only real cure for a lonely heart. Perhaps "loneliness is God's way of letting us know that it is time to reach out [to Him]."[2]

When We Seek Solitude

How easy it is to wander away from God! We don't mean to; we just get tangled up with everyday life and its disappointments and demands. The pain of fresh loneliness can bring us back quickly into the waiting arms of God.

As we escape to the Lord, the quiet of loneliness can become a prayer in itself. Loneliness becomes solitude and solitude becomes prayer.

Several months ago, feeling frustrated with the busyness of life, feeling weary with the overwhelming burdens of responsibility, and feeling isolated and lonely, I decided to start spending much more time alone with the Lord. In fact, I decided to organize my whole day around my prayer and fellowship time with God.

The new schedule worked well. I rose very early in the mornings, sometimes as early as 3:30 or 4:00. I headed for the mountains near our home to pray and read Scripture.

I drove to the top of a mountain, parked my car, and had a quiet time with the Lord. I gazed at the stars and thanked my Creator. Sometimes I stared in silence and awe at the magnificent sunrise.

The morning soon became my favorite time of the whole day. I found I wanted to give God my best hours, my most awake and creative hours. During the day I found too many interruptions. In the evenings I was too tired to listen, to read, and to concentrate.

There was something exciting, mysterious, and awesome about the early morning when all was dark and quiet and the world around me slept.

I felt a special oneness with Christ as I sat in my warm car in the chill and dampness of the early morning, high on a mountaintop awaiting sunrise, and read in the Scriptures of the many times Jesus rose early and went into the mountains to pray. I looked forward to our early morning conversation.

I remember the morning that I felt unusually lonely. In deepest thought, I sat in my car and poured out my feelings of loneliness on paper.

Lord, there is this loneliness I feel . . . a sort of inherent loneliness that won't go away. Do all human creatures feel this? I wonder. It's like a yearning to be at home . . . home with my Creator. It's an emptiness I can't really describe, can't put my finger on, can't put into words. But it's always in me, in some form or another. It's a longing I feel deep within my heart and it comes most vividly when I see a sunrise or hear the early morning song of a sparrow or watch the ocean's waves roll to the shore or feel the warm summer breeze on my face after a storm.

Lord, I've found that nothing can really satisfy this soul hunger I feel for home, not husband, children, parents, or friends. You've given me these people, and I love them. They are special gifts that help fend off the loneliness, but the creature I am yearns to be in Your tender arms. I am my Creator's child, and I long for the perfect companionship that will last forever.

How I look forward to coming home, Lord! Oh, it's not a cop-out, not an escape route when the responsibilities of life become overwhelming and when my work becomes exhausting or when the pace just won't slow down. It's a genuine craving to be with You, Lord, a craving You planted in my heart before it beat its first beat. How I look forward to an eternity with You, Lord, for You know me throughout, and You tell me that You love me . . . even when I stumble, fall, and fail.

I don't understand how You could love me, Lord, but I thank You. I love You, and I need You.

You tell me You have a home waiting for me. You tell me to stay in the race for a while longer, then I can come home. "Do the work I've given you to do," You tell me. "And when you are finished, I'll bring you home to live with Me . . . forever." I'm looking forward to "forever," Lord.

The Lord fills my discouraged heart with encouraging words on those early mornings I spend with Him. How desperately we need to share His promise with all the world's Marys who are lonely and who have lost hope.

Fellowship with God

God created us to commune with Him, to love Him, to know Him. Only in our fellowship with God do we find and know great joy. Even when life dumps its bills, disappointments, frustrations, and demands on us, we can live with God's joy filling our hearts.

I used to think of spending time alone with God as an opportunity to refuel so that I could better get on with life. Now I know that prayer and intimate communion with our Maker is not a pit stop to refresh and refuel. Prayer, communion, and fellowship with God is life itself, the reason for our existence.

I know that babies need their diapers changed, hungry families must eat, deadlines must be met, mortgages must be paid, and groceries must be bought.

But isn't life in the Lord our true priority? We were created to glorify God and to enjoy Him forever. Sure, we have our responsibilities. While most of what we do is important and must be done, may we never lose sight of why we were created. May we tell hurting women everywhere of our chief purpose—to glorify God and enjoy Him forever.

The Walking Bird

One morning during my daily walk, I saw a bird walking along the ground. Nothing was unusual about that. A lot of birds greet me in the early mornings.

But they fly; they don't walk.

Maybe this was a tired bird, or a bird with a bad wing, or a bird who had lost her song. For the entire time I watched her, she walked with great effort on those awkward spindle legs. She never did take off and fly.

Finally, in frustration, I spoke. "Bird," I said aloud, looking around to make sure no one else could hear me. "Why do you walk when God gave you wings to fly?"

Perhaps it is the same with life. We have been given the gift of prayer with our Creator. Yet we get so bogged down with the concerns of everyday life and everyday trivia that we forget that we were made to fly, not walk. We walk when we could run, even soar, through our day.

Just imagine, the One who hung the moon, who placed those brilliant stars, and who keeps this world spinning in space, gives you and me the gift of communication with Him. God has given us wings of prayer. Yet how easy it is to accept the ordinary when the extraordinary is within our reach. It's so easy to forget who we are, whose we are, and what we were made to do.

The Bread of Life

We must tell hurting women that life is good, for some have forgotten. But we must also agree that we can keenly feel the pain of loss. Each new loss brings its own painful kind of loneliness.

Let us remind them, however, that we don't face the loss alone. We can turn to the One Who tells us, "I am the bread of life. He who comes to me will never go hungry, and he who believes in me will never be thirsty" (John 6:35).

We can share intimate moments with the Savior. He waits for us to come to Him. He waits for us to come back to Him whenever we drift away. Once we truly discover Him, nothing else, no one else, can ever be as important to us.

> What we need first and foremost are intimate moments with the Savior . . . time spent all alone with Him, watching His model, listening to His counsel, feeling His touch. We need some way to connect our temporal world with His eternal perspective.[3]

St. Augustine said it so beautifully: "For Thou hast made us for Thyself, and our heart can find no rest until it rests in Thee."

Indeed, our hearts will be lonely until they find rest again in close intimate fellowship with our Lord Jesus Christ.

Intercessory Prayer

Above and beyond any other way you and I can reach out to hurting women today, we can reach out to them with prayer. When we pray for them, we tell them that we dearly love them, that we care, that we share their struggle. We speak their language. We understand. When we pray for them, we bow before God on their behalf. When we pray for them, Jesus joins us in our prayers for them. We will see a miracle happen in their lives. Jesus can reach out to them with the close comfort of His friendship, and with eternal prayers that will forever bring them peace and joy.

Such is the power within our grasp as you and I reach out with prayer to those women who suffer.

Jesus can bring them new life. "Come out!" Jesus calls to them and to us, as He called to Lazarus long ago. And we leave our tombs of despair and hopelessness; we step forward with new life, with new purpose in Christ.

---

[1]Myron S. Augsburger, *When Reason Fails* (Wheaton: Tyndale House Publishers, Inc., 1968), 75.
[2]Billy Graham, "Are You Lonely?" *Decision* (June 1988), 3.
[3](In the Foreword by Chuck Swindoll) Ken Gire, *Intimate Moments with the Savior* (Grand Rapids: Zondervan Publishing House, 1989), XI.

Questions for Reflection and Discussion

1. Have you ever been lonely? What did you do about it? What would you now tell others who are lonely?

2. What is the cure for loneliness? How can we make loneliness into a time of solitude and prayer? What is your personal definition of solitude?

3. Why is it important to have a regular daily prayer time and place? Do you personally give prayer the importance Jesus teaches us to give it? Have you developed the habit of getting alone with God each day at a regular time and place?

4. Think about and discuss the statement by Myron S. Augsburger: "Paradoxical as it may seem, the true cure for loneliness is to get alone with God, to allow one's self to rest in him. Loneliness is corrected by a sense of belonging to God."

5. Read below Jesus' prayer in John 17. For whom does He pray? How does He pray? How did the disciples react to His prayer for them? How do you react to His prayer for you?

> Father, the time has come. Glorify your Son, that your Son may glorify you. For you granted him authority over all people that he might give eternal life

to all those you have given him. Now this is eternal life: that they may know you, the only true God, and Jesus Christ, whom you have sent. I have brought you glory on earth by completing the work you gave me to do. And now, Father, glorify me in your presence with the glory I had with you before the world began.

I have revealed you to those whom you gave me out of the world. They were yours; you gave them to me and they have obeyed your word. Now they know that everything you have given me comes from you. For I gave them the words you gave me and they accepted them. They knew with certainty that I came from you, and they believed that you sent me. I pray for them. I am not praying for the world, but for those you have given me, for they are yours. All I have is yours, and all you have is mine. And glory has come to me through them. I will remain in the world no longer, but they are still in the world, and I am coming to you. Holy Father, protect them by the power of your name—the name you gave me—so that they may be one as we are one. While I was with them, I protected them and kept them safe by that name you gave me. None has been lost except the one doomed to destruction so that Scripture would be fulfilled.

I am coming to you now, but I say these things while I am still in the world, so that they may have the full measure of my joy within them. I have given them your word and the world has hated them, for they are not of the world any more than I am of the world. My prayer is not that you take them out of the world but that you protect them from the evil one. They are not of the world, even as I am not of it. Sanctify them by the truth; your word is truth. As you sent me into the world, I have sent them into the world. For them I sanctify myself, that they too may be truly sanctified.

My prayer is not for them alone. I pray also for those who will believe in me through their message, that all of them may be one, Father, just as you are in me and I am in you. May they also be in us so that the world may believe that you have sent me. I have given them the glory that you gave me, that they may be one as we are one: I in them and you in me. May they be brought to complete unity to let the world know that you sent me and have loved them even as you have loved me.

Father, I want those you have given me to be with me where I am, and to see my glory, the glory you have given me because you loved me before the creation of the world.

Righteous Father, though the world does not know you, I know you, and they know that you have sent me. I have made you known to them, and will continue to make you known in order that the love you have for me may be in them and that I myself may be in them (John 17).

6. Have Christian women in general, and have you in particular, worked to bring about unity with the Father and with others? Why or why not?

7. Discuss the following: "Jesus made prayer and fellowship with the Father the priority in His life." In what ways did Jesus make prayer a priority in His life? In what ways can we incorporate His example into our own lives? How can we help other women to realize the priority of prayer in their lives?

8. St. Augustine said: "For Thou hast made us for Thyself, and our heart can find no rest until it rests in Thee." Discuss the meaning of his statement. Have you experienced a time when you found rest in God during a troubling time?

9. James 1:2 tells us, "consider it pure joy . . . when you face trials of many kinds." How can we be joyful when we feel bereaved, sad, lonely, hopeless? Is it possible? How can we help a hurting woman once again find her joy in the Lord?

10. How can we best reach out with prayer to Christian women who suffer? You may choose to begin a prayer ministry in your church to begin reaching out to others in prayer.

Prayer

To close your personal devotional time or your group time, you may want to use the following prayer:

Father, help us to reach out to hurting women first and foremost with prayer.

Help us as we tell hurting women today about the gift of prayer, and the beauty of fellowship with the Father who loves them more than they could ever know.

Help them to know that God is just a heart's whisper away, that He yearns for us to seek His presence, that the Father reaches out to them with the gift of prayerful fellowship.

Show us how to live our own lives in prayer so that we might be useful to You in Your service.

In Jesus' name. Amen.

Chapter 3: Lonely Beaches, Broken Hearts

The Heart Can Begin Again: Reaching Out with Compassion

Helping Women Wounded by Discouragement

Bible Study: Read Luke 13:10–13

Only Luke's Gospel mentions the woman who had spent 18 years staring at the floor, unable to stand up, sit down, or straighten her crooked back.

Jesus and His disciples traveled through her city on their way from Galilee to Judea. On the Sabbath, as was His custom, Jesus entered the synagogue. She, too, entered the synagogue, and must have had to ignore pointing fingers and curious eyes. When Jesus saw her, He felt deep compassion. He reached out and touched her. Jesus healed her, even though healing on the Sabbath was against Mosaic law. When the ruler of the synagogue rebuked Jesus, He firmly exposed the inconsistency of those who would lead an ox to water on the Sabbath, yet who opposed the healing of this woman.

That Sabbath, Jesus also did something that made the religious leaders cringe. He referred to the woman as "a daughter of Abraham" (v. 16), a description reserved for the prestigious "sons" of Abraham. Before the upright religious folk, Jesus gave her a high place of honor when He affirmed that she, too, belonged to the family of Abraham.

Compassion. Deep compassion.

We want to warn Him: "Jesus, You will pay dearly for Your many acts of compassion. You will soon be nailed to a cross by the very ones who cringe at Your actions in the synagogue. But a cross can't stop Your compassion. For You will also reach out with forgiving compassion to those who will drive the nails through Your hands and feet, to those who will scourge Your chest and back, to those who will spit at You and mock You while You breathe Your final breath."

Jesus knew, but compassion was worth the price He would pay.

We haven't finished the woman's story. Something wonderful happened to her when Jesus touched her compassionately. Something totally unexpected. For the first time in 18 years, she straightened her back, stretched to her full height. We can imagine that while the sons of Abraham hung their heads in shame, she held her head high. And from that day on, we can imagine that this daughter of Abraham never missed another sunrise, sunset, or star-studded sky.

After 18 years, the woman surely must have felt defeated by life and lost hope of ever becoming whole again. But then Jesus came. His compassion restored health to her body and hope to her heart.

The Greatest Enemy

We live in a world where many Christian women have lost hope. We meet and touch them every day.

Brokenness meets us on all sides: marriages, homes, relationships, dreams. For many women, life seems a continual cycle of brokenness and loss. They lose their loved ones, their vocations, their ambitions, and their youth. The cycle of loss is a part of everyday living and often leads to despair, the greatest enemy of the believer's heart.

Many women around us are encumbered with guilt and disturbed by painful pasts. Many are hurt by sickness, crushed by loss and failure, and wearied from seemingly fruitless waiting.

Many women are discouraged and confused; many have lost their jubilation. Life moves forward so quickly we seldom have adequate time to contemplate and reflect. In the race of life, we give our hurting hearts little time, little reflection for healing and insightful understanding. Running from one activity to another, Christian women can easily lose perspective and forget that we race toward a finish line, the home that awaits us as believers in Christ. If we aren't alert, our hearts—the home of the Holy Spirit—can lose the laughter and joy of belonging to the family of God.

The White-gabled House

Whenever I see the white-gabled house on Rocky Ridge Road, I am reminded of how easily life's crises and problems can smother the gladness and delight of our hearts as they rest in God.

Day after day, the workmen built the great Victorian-style house. The magnificent house sat on a lovely spot surrounded by large green yards and mature trees. When the house was finished, the construction crew packed their gear, and the builder put up a sign in the front lawn: "For Sale."

Not long after, a large family with happy, playing children moved in. Soon pink begonia bloomed in the side gardens, tricycles and toys covered the stone walk, a pair of rocking chairs graced the front porch, and a new tire swing draped an old oak tree.

In the evenings, the soft lights within made the house seem to glow. I could imagine a contented growing family sharing a quiet evening together around the fireplace.

The house was no longer empty. It had come alive with the laughter and joy of family togetherness. The house sheltered a family. The house had become a home.

But Then . . . Something Happened

One day a construction crew pulled up beside the house and started work on a massive electrical facility. Several months later, the completed gray complex cast its shadows across the white-gabled house.

Soon the lights inside were off and the house was empty. Gone were the tricycles and toys from the walk, the rocking chairs, and tire swing. The pink begonia wilted from lack of care. Taped onto the tall front Victorian window hung a red-lettered sign: "For Sale. Property of Central Bank."

It was a sad sight, as if the house somehow had died. The life inside had vanished. It seemed a hollow shell where laughter, joy, and family once lived.

Do Not Lose Heart

What happened to the house on Rocky Ridge Road is not unlike what can happen to Christian women. We are all like the empty house until we give our hearts and lives to God through Jesus Christ. God, the Holy Spirit, moves into our "house" and we take on signs of new life. God brings to our home laughter, joy, and familial fellowship with Him. We seem to glow with the light of the One who illumines our lives and enriches them with eternal meaning. We enjoy quiet evenings in rich fellowship with Him. Jesus Christ becomes our lives, and we begin to grow in our exciting newfound faith.

Who knows what kind of shadow can fall across the Christian woman's path and cause her to lose her laughter, joy, and fellowship with Christ? Perhaps a tragedy, loss, or heartbreak can cause her to despair. In her desperation, she sometimes gives up on life. When she does, it is as if something within her has died. Her inner light no longer shines brightly. The rich, full fellowship she once shared now seems empty.

As believers, however, we don't lose our places in God's family, our salvation. Once we genuinely have accepted Christ's invitation and have become daughters in God's family, we always will be His children. That is God's promise to you, to me, and to all those who believe and accept His gift of grace and life.

"God began doing a good work in you," Paul wrote. "And He will continue it until it is finished when Jesus Christ comes again" (Phil. 1:6 NCV).

We don't lose our relationships, but certainly we can lose our joy and fellowship.

It's not a new problem among Christians. The apostle Paul saw it happen, too. He saw the despair among the early believers who were persecuted by the Roman government for following Christ. Many quickly lost heart and gave up. Paul wrote lengthy, loving letters to encourage them and to tell them not to lose heart even when they were beaten down. He told them to remember Jesus Christ and to look to the hope and glory that awaited them (see 2 Cor. 4:17).

I know firsthand about broken hearts. At times, I have lost the laughter, joy, and fellowship with Christ that I so love and lean on. During those times I thought God had deserted me. He seemed nowhere around me. It seemed my prayers would no longer reach Him. My heart in turmoil could find no rest and peace.

I remember the early Saturday morning my beloved grandmother, "Mama," died. It was a turning point in my life. Mama and I were so close. We loved each other as much as a granddaughter and grandmother could ever love. From my birth, Mama tucked me into the high, quilt-covered bed and told me stories about Jesus and His love for me. She and my grandfather nurtured me in the Christian faith. How I loved them and appreciated them for their faithful devotion to me!

The Old Yellow Porch Swing

Whenever I relive that early Saturday morning, the old yellow porch swing comes to mind. Before Mama's death, I would sit in the swing for hours, I would look out beyond the trees and small flower garden and contemplate God's goodness, His love for me, and my gratefulness to Him. The swing was a happy place for me; it was the secret spot where God and I often met.

But all that changed the Saturday morning my beautiful grandmother died. Since I was only 10 days away from giving birth to my daughter, I couldn't attend the funeral 300 miles away. My doctor told me the long trip would be too uncomfortable and too risky.

All that day, I sat in the porch swing and cried. In fact, I cried all the next week. The laughter, joy, and fellowship that had become symbolic of the porch swing had disappeared. Instead, I shouted angry questions at God. "Why, God, did you let Mama die before my daughter was born? Why couldn't you let Mama live just 10 more days to see her precious new great-granddaughter?"

Mama had so looked forward to Alyce's birth. She had hoped to live long enough to cuddle her tiny namesake in her arms as she had once held and cuddled me and my firstborn son. I couldn't understand why God allowed what seemed to me such cruel timing.

Ten days later, still sad and brokenhearted, I went into Caesarean surgery. At one point in the surgical preparations, my crying overwhelmed me. My doctor stopped and asked me if I felt physical pain. I shook my head. "No," I wanted to tell him, "physical pain couldn't hurt half as much as this pain in my heart."

I felt no particular closeness to God the week between Mama's death and my surgery. Little did I know that even when I thought God was far away from me, He was still at work, loving, healing, and restoring my broken heart.

I was soon to discover God's love for me anew. Late that Tuesday morning, when I returned to my room from surgery, He placed into my tired arms a beautiful healthy newborn daughter. My very own Alyce.

New life pierced the gloom in my heart. New life cut through the devastating shroud of death that had surrounded me. God blessed me with a new Alyce, not one to take Mama's place, but one to carry on her name and memory. I knew that whenever I looked at my daughter's face or called her name, I would think of my grandmother.

Immediately, my heart overflowed with tenderness, joy, and thankfulness. I breathed a heartfelt prayer of renewed fellowship with God. Once again, as I lay still in that hospital bed nursing my newborn daughter, I felt God close to me.

The Heart Can Begin Again

I know the heart can begin again. Even when we are engulfed by troubles and don't know what to do, even when the pain inside is more than we can stand, God doesn't leave us. He stays beside us, working all things toward our good and the good of His kingdom. God is always as close as a prayer. Through all our painful ordeals, God never stops whispering His words of love, encouragement, and hope to our weary hearts. "We know that in all things God works for the good of those who love him, who have been called according to his purpose" (Rom. 8:28). That is God's promise to you and me.

Our Triumph

No doubt, when Jesus' closest friends climbed to the mountaintops with Him, listened to Him tell wonderful stories about God's kingdom, and sat around the fire talking long into the night, they could not have imagined what the future would bring. They knew Jesus personally, and shared a rare friendship.

Then that ominous Friday came, and in their unexpected terror, they scattered. They watched their beloved friend slapped, spit upon, abused, and finally executed by Roman soldiers. All their dreams for the future seemed shattered. Their hearts broken, they lost hope.

They spent a sad Saturday morning enveloped by the darkness of death, crying for their dear friend, and wondering why God allowed this terrible tragedy.

Then Sunday Dawned

The disciples and friends of Jesus thought that dark Saturday would last forever. Never had they felt so sorrowful. They had lost their hope. Jesus, their Lord and friend, was dead and buried.

But God had other plans. When Mary Magdalene walked to Jesus' grave in the predawn hours, she didn't find a dead Jesus there. Instead she heard Jesus call her name! Sunday had dawned bright with the resurrected Christ. Mary's sad heart filled with hope and became jubilant again. She ran to the disciples to share the good news. "I have seen the Lord!" she proclaimed.

Did the mourning, weeping disciples believe Mary? No! "When they heard that Jesus was alive and that [Mary] had seen him, they did not believe it" (Mark 16:11). Only when Jesus appeared personally to the disciples, pointed out His pierced hands and feet, ate with them, and then "opened their minds so they could understand the Scriptures" (Luke 24:45), did they finally believe Jesus had risen.

Once the disciples were convinced, resurrection filled their hearts. They were never again the same. For they, too, had seen the Lord.

True, we may have troubles all around us, but we are never defeated. We often don't know what to do, but we cannot give up. We are often persecuted, but God never leaves us.

We hurt sometimes, but we are never destroyed. God is always close to us in all our trying circumstances.

What do we do when our hearts are filled with heaviness, encumbered with guilt, disturbed by painful pasts? What do we do when we are wounded by sickness, crushed by loss and failure, and wearied from seemingly fruitless waiting? What do we do when our hearts are tired and confused and have lost their jubilation?

We trust. We continue to trust the One who has promised to stay close to us and to work our troubles for good (see Rom. 8:28). God, through His Son, Jesus Christ, reaches out to us and forgives, helps us to overcome sorrowful pasts, brings rest from our sickness, carries us through loss and failure, and gives us vision and hope in our waiting.

A troubled or broken heart can become a heart at peace again. God can stir the cold ashes of our despondent lives and make them glow anew with laughter and joy and renewed family fellowship.

Won't you share this lesson with a woman who needs to hear it?

Questions for Reflection and Discussion

1. Describe a person you know who has lost heart, who has lost joy in the Lord, who has forgotten just how much God loves her. How can you and I, as individuals and as a church, minister to her? Why is it important that we do so?

2. Have you ever experienced a situation or a time in your life when you thought God seemed far away? Have you ever felt that God didn't hear your prayers? Describe it.

3. Think about and discuss this statement: "The cycle of loss is a part of everyday living, and loss can often lead to despair, the greatest enemy of the believer's heart."

   Why is despair the "greatest enemy of the believer's heart"?

4. Do you believe that "the heart can begin again"? What does this statement mean to you?

5. Discuss this statement by the apostle Paul: "God began doing a good work in you. And He will continue it until it is finished when Jesus Christ comes again" (Phil. 1:6 NCV).

6. If time permits, write a letter to a woman you know who needs a word of hope in her life. Reach out to her with compassion,

just as Jesus reached out to the woman with the crooked back. Let her know you care.

Prayer

To close your personal devotional time or your group time, you may want to use the following prayer:

O Lord, just as You reached out to the bent-over woman and gave her new hope and new purpose, reach out to us, and allow us to reach out to hurting women. Teach us by Your example how to reach out with compassion.

Thank You, dear Lord, for the wounds that You endured at Calvary for us. May we always be grateful to You. May we always remember the price You paid so that we could rest in the new hope You provide. In Jesus' precious name we pray. Amen.

Chapter 4: The Heart Can Begin Again

An Alabaster Flask of Perfume: Reaching Out with Affirmation

Helping Victims of Spouse Abuse

Bible Study: Read Luke 7:36–50

She was a woman who must have lost her sense of self. Mistreated by the people in her daily life, she undoubtedly carried a heavy heart and felt worthless. How urgently she must have needed a word of affirmation, a reason to be alive, a purpose, and a peace.

Scripture refers to her as a sinner—no name, just a sinner. She probably was a prostitute who did business on the streets of Nain, a village of southwest Galilee.

The religious Pharisees must have despised her. Can you imagine how upset they were when she entered the home of Simon the Pharisee uninvited? Simon was hosting a men's dinner party for Jesus that evening. No self-respecting woman would burst into a room full of men.

But she did. She must have felt she had nothing to lose. She held an alabaster flask of perfume. Upon seeing Jesus, she dropped at His feet and began to cry. Her tears poured onto His feet, washing from them the dust and dirt of Galilee's streets. She then wiped His feet clean with her long hair and kissed them. She broke the flask of treasured fragrance and anointed His feet with tenderness and love.

By this time, Simon, the host, had seen enough. He scolded her with harsh, critical words. Simon even questioned Jesus' integrity for allowing such a woman to touch Him.

But Jesus could see through her tarnished reputation. He could see the woman's heart, a heart that sought forgiveness and purpose in life. Her heart cried out for a kind word.

The Pharisees must have felt horror and surprise when Jesus did not criticize the woman. He did not seem offended. He did not push her away. Instead, Jesus affirmed her in front of the room filled with narrow-sighted men.

"Do you see this woman?" Jesus asked Simon. "I came into your house. You did not give me any water for my feet, but she wet my feet with her tears and wiped them with her hair" (v. 44).

Jesus continued, "You did not give me a kiss, but this woman, from the time I entered, has not stopped kissing my feet. You did not put oil on my head, but she has poured perfume on my feet" (vv. 45–46). Without apology, Simon had neglected these elementary gestures of hospitality.

Then Jesus astounded them all and, no doubt, left the men speechless. "Therefore, I tell you, her many sins have been forgiven—for she loved much" (v. 47).

A sudden hush must have swept the room. Can you imagine the men's reaction, too shocked to speak?

In the moment of quiet, Jesus turned to the woman who still knelt by His feet. Perhaps He smiled at her. Perhaps Jesus took her hand in His and brought her to her feet so that she could stand before Him and look Him in the eye.

"Your sins are forgiven," He told her. "Your faith has saved you." Then Jesus spoke three more words that would no doubt remain within her heart and memory for the rest of her life: "Go in peace" (vv. 48, 50). Jesus forgave her and affirmed her. On the streets of Galilee, she no longer would be referred to as the sinner. Jesus had restored her sense of self. She became known from that day as the "woman who loved much," the woman Jesus honored.

The nameless woman who entered Simon's house in pain departed in peace. Not only did Jesus publicly forgive her, but He publicly affirmed her. The woman who bowed down, cleaned, kissed, and anointed Jesus' feet departed that day with a freshly cleansed heart and a brand-new life.

Do You See this Woman?

Do you see the hurting women who weave in and out of your day? She may be the woman at the checkout counter or the driver of the car next to yours. She may be the mother sitting on the edge of the community swimming pool with her young son. She may be your mother, grandmother, daughter, or granddaughter. She may be the woman who sits beside you at church or your neighbor down the street.

Look closely at her, for she is a hurting woman, a woman mistreated by the people in her daily life. She carries a heavy heart and feels worthless. As God's heart and God's hands to a hurting world, we must reach out to her with affirmation.

Margaret's Story

Margaret was a lovely Christian woman with silver-streaked hair, a petite figure, and a gentle, warm smile. She had a certain sophistication about her, a natural charm. Yet beneath her appearance was a woman who had endured a life no one deserves.

Margaret had finished school and married. Together she and her new husband set up a home, had a son, and looked forward to a storybook marriage.

Within a few years, for no apparent or predictable reason, Margaret's husband began to abuse her. Physically. Emotionally. Verbally. What began as a once-in-a-while slap became routine, life-threatening beatings, beatings that left her scarred outside and inside, beatings that destroyed her self-esteem.

With little support from her family, Margaret endured the beatings for as long as she could. She tried to be a loving wife and a good Christian mother. She tried desperately to hold her deteriorating marriage together, hiding her terrible secret.

But she couldn't do it. The beatings were too brutal. She feared for her life and the life of her young son. Her heart broken, her dreams shattered, Margaret's marriage ended in divorce.

The Problem of Domestic Violence

Margaret's story is becoming a common one. Look at the women around you. Many homes today are not what God intended. Instead of a place where love and acceptance are the norm, violence and abuse are everyday experiences.

Are you shocked? I am.

Domestic abuse knows no boundaries. Educational background, income, class, race, or faith seem to make little difference. Our society was shocked by the discovered beatings of Nicole Simpson by her husband. Most of America stayed glued to their televisions during the O. J. Simpson murder trial. Many women are suffering in secret and in silence around this country and, indeed, around the world.

Society has long known about spouse abuse, but fear, embarrassment, and practical concerns covered it with a blanket of silence. Today we are becoming aware of the unbelievable frequency and seriousness of spouse abuse.

These statistics may surprise you. In the United States:

- The type of man who is most likely to batter witnessed parental violence as a child, acts violently toward his children, and needs to control or dominate females.
- More than 4,000 women—about 30 percent of all female homicide victims—die of domestic abuse each year.
- According to the National Coalition Against Domestic Violence, more than 3 million women in the US are battered each year. Christian families are not immune.
- When deaths from the violence occur, in 85 to 90 percent of the cases police had been called to the home for domestic violence at least once during the two years before the killing; in more than half the cases, police had been called five or more times. Often when the woman reports the case to police, the attacker becomes more violent.
- Violence is 14 times more likely to occur after the parties separate. Separation or divorce may only increase the attacker's anger because the woman is no longer under his power.

One of the Best-kept Secrets

Spouse abuse is as intense a problem in the body of Christ as it is outside the church. In other words, a Margaret may be sitting beside you on the church pew on any given Sunday morning. It's unbelievable and frightening. Violence appears to be growing even among churchgoing families.

What does spouse abuse include? Slaps, kicks, and other forms of physical battering; sexual assault; rape; and even murder. Causing emotional pain with destructive put-downs, threats, or name-calling also is abuse. Abuse can be spousal neglect or "the silent syndrome"—consistently ignoring the spouse or failing to communicate or bond in relationship.

The male batterer may come from a violent home. He often blames others for his problems or denies he has a problem. He may use drinking and wife-beating to cope with stress.

The abused wife often tries to keep peace in the family at all costs. She is overly trusting of others, and assumes the guilt for her husband's abusive behavior. She feels helpless and hopeless to stop the violence, and as a result often suffers from feelings of worthlessness.

Margaret's Life after Divorce

After Margaret's divorce, she and her son were left financially hurting, a common occurrence among today's newly divorced women. Society has begun to call them "the new poor." As a single mother with few financial resources and memories of the humiliating experience of battering, Margaret suffered from low self-esteem and a severe lack of confidence. She feared a future that looked sad, scary, and hopeless.

Then Margaret met her prince. Stephen, a widower, was tall, attractive, financially stable, and a skilled surgeon. Stephen offered her a strong shoulder to cry on, a deep respect for her personhood, and a sympathetic ear that listened with patience.

Everyone liked Stephen. He was a kind, caring, gentle man. He held an important leadership role in his church. Stephen was esteemed by many devoted patients. He was almost too good to be true.

Within nine months after her divorce, Stephen offered Margaret a beautiful life and a hope-filled future as his wife. Margaret was thrilled. It seemed like a dream come true. Margaret would no longer journey through life alone but with a kind Christian man who would love her, affirm her, and help her find her lost sense of self. Margaret accepted his proposal of marriage. She began to feel hope and renewal within her tired heart.

For the first two weeks, Margaret lived a blissful life as Stephen's wife, growing from the nourishment he gave her, basking in the sunshine of his love for her. But then the happily-ever-after storybook marriage became a living nightmare.

Margaret remembers: "As I was changing our bed, I dropped the dirty sheets on the floor—not the clean sheets, the dirty sheets! For no apparent reason, Stephen became enraged. I was shocked! That's the day I discovered Stephen's violent temper."

The battering began. Margaret's sense of hope and happiness was smothered by bewilderment and despair. Stephen began by hitting Margaret, and the violence intensified. He would throw her against furniture, grab her hair, and shove her to the floor. Stephen used the same violent attacks on Margaret that she had, in confidence, told him her first husband used to hurt her.

Neighbors could hear Margaret's screams during the frequent beatings and sometimes gathered on the street beneath the bedroom window. "They knew what was going on," Margaret said, "but no one knew what to do. And no one wanted to get involved."

Stephen was liked and respected in the church where he had been a lifetime member. In spite of routine beatings, Margaret devoted herself to Stephen and to his church. She told no one in the church about the abuse. And no one seemed to suspect it.

"Stephen was careful to bruise only the parts of my body and legs that my clothes would hide," Margaret said.

After a beating to the head, Margaret suffered permanent hearing loss in one ear. Her doctor wrote "trauma-caused" on her chart.

Margaret also endured severe emotional abuse. Stephen called her names, tapped the home phone, and allowed her little contact with family or friends.

Margaret stayed married to Stephen and endured his abuse for 15 years. "People often ask me why I didn't leave him, why I stayed with him so long," Margaret said. "During those years, I felt so alone, alienated, and worthless. I lost the will to live. I was so under Stephen's control, I couldn't even think for myself. I felt as though I didn't belong to the human race."

Margaret tried several times to kill herself but each time she failed. She later found out that Stephen had also battered his first wife, Sandra. After 20 years of daily abuse, Sandra committed suicide.

Several years into the marriage, Stephen became even more hostile. "I was so terrified of him, I moved into the guest bedroom and had a deadbolt lock put on my door," Margaret said. "I really believed my life was in danger."

Shattered Dreams

Perhaps you know someone who is hiding the terrible secret of spouse abuse. She lives from day to day in fear, confusion, and despair. Beating after beating, she is being destroyed. As a girl she dreamed of a happy marriage with the man she loved. She wanted everything a home represents: love, trust, honesty, companionship, compassion, faithfulness, strong loving arms to embrace her, a secure shelter from the world, and a warm nest in which to rear her children. But the pain of battering has left her dream in shambles. She feels unsafe and unloved in her own home, and she is ready to give up. She doesn't know what to do. She keeps hoping the abuse will stop and things at home will get better. But after so many promises, after so much pain, she quickly is losing heart and hope.

The walls of many homes hide hurting women who are terrified of their husbands and afraid for their children. They are women who have lost heart, who have lost the will to live. They are the women who sit around you and me in church on Sunday mornings living lives of physical and emotional abuse. They wear long-sleeved blouses in summer to cover their bruises and cuts. They secretly cry for help.

You and I need to reach out to these women. As sisters in Christ, as members of His body, we all share the problem of battering. When one member hurts, other members hurt as well. When one member is wounded, we all cringe in pain. We cannot function properly as a Christian body when even one of us is being crippled by another's violent hand.

How can you and I reach out to abused women? We can reach out in several ways. First, we need to help her remove herself and her children from the hostile environment. We can recommend good Christian attorneys and counselors, people who know what to do and how to do it. We can become aware of shelters in our communities and volunteer to work at local domestic abuse centers. We can also contribute to the financial support of victims.

Second, we need to let the abused woman know that someone cares for her, that she is created by God as a person of infinite worth. She does not need to be pitied but empowered to become all that God intended her to be. Your support as a friend and as a church can do much to help her regain her feeling of worth. In that way, you and I can reach out to her in the same way Jesus reached out—with affirmation.

It's not easy to reach out to a woman who desperately hides the secret of spouse abuse. We often feel it's none of our business, and it's uncomfortable to approach another in pain. Sometimes if our suspicions aren't confirmed, we become embarrassed. But we must reach out. The wounded woman needs God's heart and God's hands to bring her back to her feet, to look at life with hope and self-confidence. Without intervention, the abuse will not stop. In most cases the abuse will accelerate.

A Hopeless Future?

Margaret was the victim of two violent, abusive marriages. For many years, she believed the future held no hope for her, but Margaret's turning point came. Margaret finally found hope.

After an unusually tense confrontation with Stephen, fearing for her life, Margaret worked up the courage to call an attorney friend. With the attorney's help, Margaret was able to leave the abusive home. She also stopped going to Stephen's church. Soon, a friend reached out and invited Margaret to her church. The members were kind and welcomed her with open arms. Margaret felt at home.

"That's what I needed most," Margaret remembers, "a friend who affirmed me, who reached out to me with understanding. I will be eternally grateful to her."

During the last three years at the church, Margaret has found the support, encouragement, and emotional healing she so desperately needed. Her self-esteem is growing. When she thought no one cared, Christian women reached out to her.

"My Sunday School class members call me and make me feel like a part of the church. They listen to me and make me feel that someone really cares. When I had minor surgery, my pastor and some members greeted me at the hospital. I feel surrounded by the church's love and prayers. It's like a brand-new life."

The Haunting Question

Within the noise and chaos of everyday life, within the echo of criticism and harsh words, within the pain and terror that many women suffer today, Jesus stops, looks at you and me, and asks: "Do you see this woman?"

(Some names have been changed to protect the privacy of those involved.)

Questions for Reflection and Discussion

1. What factors in our society contribute to domestic violence? Can we do anything to reduce or eliminate these factors?

2. After years of abuse, Margaret described herself this way: "During those years, I felt so alone, alienated, and worthless. I lost the will to live. I was so under Stephen's control, I couldn't even think for myself. I felt like I didn't belong to the human race." How do you think physical, emotional, verbal, and mental spouse abuse can devastate a person's self-image?

3. Do you think that spouse abuse is too delicate an issue for Christians to intervene? How should you and I deal with a spouse abuse situation we discover in our church or community?

4. Why should you and I refer the abused woman to a Christian attorney and/or counselor?

5. What do words of affirmation do for the woman who has lost her sense of self? Can you think of a time when a friend reached out and affirmed you when you most needed affirmation?

6. Think about and discuss the following facts about spouse abuse. If you know an abused woman, give her a copy of the following letter. You may save her life.

Dear _____:

Domestic violence is a delicate issue, but I can no longer ignore the problem. Experts tell me that unless someone intervenes and the violence is stopped, what starts out as a threat, a kick, or a slap will always escalate in intensity. In many cases, a woman's life is in grave danger. In fact, 30 percent of women who are killed each year are killed by their spouses.

I also have learned that men who batter in one relationship will batter in other relationships.

Please forgive me if I am stepping into private territory, but I must take that risk. Please allow me to share some information with you.

If you are the victim of spouse abuse, seek help immediately. It is never right for someone to hurt you. Know that authorities consider physical abuse to be criminal behavior. Here are steps you can take:

- If you have been hurt or are afraid of being hurt, talk to me, a pastor, or a close friend or family member. Let us help you.
- Make yourself and your children safe. Leave the situation and go to a place of safety. Do not tell the abuser where you are staying.
- Let me help you contact a local women's shelter for support and guidance.
- If your pastor or counselor recommends marital counseling, ask him or her to counsel you separately, not together. "A couple in a battering situation need separate counseling," states Michelle McAlpine, a family violence center counselor. "The abuse is his problem, not hers. He is totally responsible for his behavior because he chooses to be abusive. She is not responsible for his behavior. It puts her at greater risk if a pastor counsels them together. A woman who is battered does not have freedom of speech."

I want to help you. Please let me help you.

If you suspect spouse abuse, do you feel comfortable sending a letter like this to the victim? Why or why not? Discuss the options.

7. If you are a friend or family member of a possible spouse abuse victim, read and discuss the following:

- Watch for the warning signs of abuse (see question 8) and alert your pastor or church/community counselor.
- If you are a close enough friend of the victim, approach her privately, definitely not in the presence of her husband. Ask some questions that will help her open up to you, such as: "Is everything all right at home?" "Is someone hurting you?" (If her answer is yes, ask: "Is your husband hurting you?")
- Don't judge or criticize her, but listen with understanding, and support her with your prayers, presence, and some concrete suggestions about what she can do.
- Put her in touch with someone who can help her, a pastor, a Christian counselor, and/or your local domestic violence center.
- If she and her children need a safe place to go, take them to a domestic violence safety center, to a family member or friend who lives in another county or state, or to the home of a volunteer in your church who is unknown to the husband and who can offer a "safe house." (Do not take her into your own home if her husband might anticipate her staying with you. Your life could be endangered.) If possible, help her financially or arrange for the church to provide her with travel and expense money.

A woman who is being beaten by a violent husband cannot remain in the home with him. The abuse will not stop. It will accelerate. Until her husband can receive the treatment he needs, she and her children must be removed from the situation.

8. Read and discuss the following spouse abuse warning signs. Become suspicious of spouse abuse if you notice a woman in your family or church or community who:

- has visible cuts, bruises, black eyes, or other injuries and her explanations are not consistent with them. For example, "I ran into a door knob and got this black eye."
- consistently misses appointments or church commitments.
- is reluctant to invite anyone to her home.
- seems on edge, jittery, withdrawn, or has frequent mood swings.

- won't stay around to talk with anyone after a luncheon, meeting, or church service because she must hurry home.
- wears unusually heavy clothing out of season, such as long sleeves in hot weather to cover bruises on her arms.
- often wears makeup heavier than usual to hide bruises or marks on her face.

9. If you are meeting with a group, covenant together to pray for God's guidance as you begin to reach out to abused women. Plan together how you can help and affirm an abused woman. Check to see what is available for women in your church and/or community. Inquire about community programs that can train women to deal directly with battered women and children. Consider starting a support group for battered women in your church.

Prayer

To close your personal devotional time or your group time, you may want to use the following prayer:

Dear Lord, we pray for the gift of intuition sensitive enough to penetrate the layers of poise, attractiveness, and charm, to see, hear, and feel the pain that so often hides behind a gentle smile and cheerful voice. We know that beneath the surface sophistication, behind the carefully controlled words and the placid facial expression may reside a tempest of pain and despair.

Help us to be able to see with Your eyes, to hear with Your ears, and to feel, to love, to affirm with Your heart. Let us be Your gentle hands in this hurting world. Draw us near to women who need our help so that we may reach out to them in Your name. Amen.

Chapter 5: An Alabaster Flask of Perfume

God's Heart, God's Hands: Reaching Out with Needed Help

Helping Victims of Childhood Sexual Abuse

Bible Study: Read Mark 5:21–34

We don't know her name. We know only that she was a woman with a dreadful secret, a secret that lived in her heart and mind every day. For 12 years she suffered with a humiliating condition in her society, a hemorrhage that caused her to bleed continuously. According to Mosaic law, the constant flow of blood made her unclean. The law prohibited her from touching or being touched. She spent everything she had on doctors who could offer no cure.

How she must have craved the warm touch of a friend's hand, a loving embrace, a husband's strong arms around her. Yet she had to remain alone, alienated from others and from life itself.

Devastated. Ashamed. Humiliated. That's how the hemorrhaging woman must have felt the day Jesus walked into her city. But wait. If she were here today, the story she would tell might be this:

I had heard about Jesus. The townspeople said Jesus could heal sick people. 'Please let it be true, God,' I had prayed that morning to the God of Abraham. Jesus was talking with an important man in the city. Jairus, I believe. Someone had said Jairus was asking Jesus to make his little daughter well. They walked in haste toward Jairus' home. On the way, however, a great crowd gathered around the two men. I guess everyone was curious about the Healer. For a moment, the Healer and Jairus were hemmed in and unable to move.

I had been standing on my feet for a long time. I could feel the blood pouring heavily from me. I worried that it might spill onto the ground. Then I saw my chance, my chance to reach out to Jesus, the Healer. "If only . . . if only . . . " I whispered under my breath as I made my way through the crowd. The law demanded I shout "unclean, unclean" when I approached others. But there was no time. I was so anxious to touch Jesus, I slipped unannounced through the swarm of people.

Trembling, I reached out and touched His clothes. Immediately I felt the flow of blood cease. I felt the power of His healing rush through me. I turned to hurry home, escape the crowd, and thank the God of Abraham for this Jesus.

But then what I feared most happened. Jesus stopped. He looked around. Somehow He knew, He knew I had touched Him.

"Who touched my clothes?" (v. 30) He asked. I knew I would be punished for touching a man of God for, in my touching Him, I had made Him ceremonially unclean. I wondered what the punishment would be. I mustered up all my courage and stepped forward. Falling at His feet, I confessed to Him the truth. Then I trembled as I awaited harsh words and my certain reproof.

To my surprise, His voice was gentle. "Daughter," He said to me. I looked up into His eyes. He called me "daughter," as if I actually belonged to Him, to His family. It had been a long time since anyone had so lovingly, so purely, called me "daughter."

He continued. "Your faith has healed you. Go in peace and be freed from your suffering" (v. 34).

Then He was gone and the crowd disappeared with Him. I stood there for a long time and pondered His words, remembered His eyes, and repeated aloud His blessing of peace.

Devastation, shame, humiliation. All of these were gone from my life. I trusted Jesus with my painful secret. I reached out to Him, and He reached back to me with the love, help, and healing I needed most.

A Humiliating Secret

We don't know her name. We only know that she was a woman with a dreadful secret. For years she had suffered with it.

Likewise, a humiliating secret lives in our contemporary society. Devastated. Ashamed. Humiliated. That's how many women feel who have experienced childhood sexual abuse. The results are severely hurting women, women who are devastated and ashamed, women who desperately need healing help.

For many years, Liz carried a heavy load of unresolved anger, fear, and loneliness. She was troubled by frightening recurring nightmares. Liz described herself as "an open wound desperately wanting to be healed but festering with anger and hate." Her childhood was stolen by her father, a man who used her selfishly, secretly for years and then abandoned her mother and family.

Liz was one of the fortunate ones, however. Liz reached out to a Christian counselor. Healing didn't happen overnight; but with the counselor's help, Liz has been able to put the terrible ordeal behind her and move forward with her life.

Childhood Sexual Abuse

Sexual abuse is unlike any other childhood abuse. It is degrading, painful, and confusing to a child. It robs a little girl of her childhood—a time that should be carefree and creative and which, once lost, never can be recovered.

Childhood sexual abuse usually leaves its young victim hurting and suffering with a deep sense of shame, guilt, and worthlessness. It can leave a lifelong scar. Those feelings are intensified when the producer of that shame and pain is the girl's father, the person who is supposed to love her, care for her, guide her spiritually, and be her strength throughout her journey to womanhood.

Only within the past few years have women begun to share this humiliating secret. Childhood sexual abuse is a form of bullying, only worse. A little girl cannot understand this terrible trauma caused by an adult she trusts. She doesn't have the maturity to grasp what is happening to her. She is at the complete mercy of someone older, bigger, smarter. An innocent little girl is no match for an adult abuser.

What Is Sexual Abuse?

Sexual abuse or *molestation* is defined as "any sexual touch by force, trickery, or bribery between two people between whom is an imbalance of age, size, power, or knowledge. The power imbalance and intimidation results in the child living with a dreaded secret."[1] Sexual abuse happens in families of all social levels, regardless of income, community prominence, or church affiliation.

Alice Huskey's Story

Alice Huskey's father began sexually abusing her when she was only three years old. The abuse continued almost daily for the next decade.

Alice came forward with her story and reached out for treatment. She then wrote about her ordeal hoping to help others who are hiding the unresolved pain of childhood sexual abuse.

Alice revealed that because of her father's angry threats on her life, she kept the dark secret inside, afraid someone would find out about it. At age 13, Alice finally decided to tell her unsuspecting mother about her father's demanding and intimidating behavior.

After telling her mother, however, Alice panicked.

"I had blurted out the secret myself!" she remembered. "There was nothing I could do now but bear the consequences. Mother reacted in shock, but managed to do the right thing. Most importantly, she believed me. And then she took action."[2]

Alice's mother confided in friends, asked their advice, and took her daughter to the sheriff's office. Not long afterward, two deputy sheriffs arrested her father. But the nightmare had only begun. The news broke quickly in her neighborhood and church community.

"It seemed as if some of my mother's friends at church were supportive," she admits, "but it was so painful to hear snatches of gossip at church and in the community. I remember going to the church picnic and wanting only to stay close to my mother. She was all I had and I needed her. I didn't want to leave her side because I was afraid. I felt as if I had a big sign around my neck saying 'dirty, ugly, naughty, guilty—stay away.'"[3]

The case came to trial. Alice described the experience in one word: "Devastating." Her father was acquitted with only a short stay in custody for observation. Her parents divorced, and Alice went to live with a foster mother. Her secret was out, and the shame, humiliation, and gossip followed her everywhere she went.

The Problem of Child Sexual Abuse

Believe it or not, "most of these children [the victims of sexual molestation] are between eight and thirteen years old, boys as well as girls. Half are molested within the family and half are molested by nonfamilial assailants."[4]

Sexual molestation is a problem not only in the secular society but within the Christian community as well. Alice Huskey points out how widespread sexual abuse is:

"In a group of four friends, one may have been abused. In a school or church classroom or Bible study of twenty, five may be victims of abuse. In a church of two hundred, fifty may be victims of abuse. In a workplace of fifty, twelve may have been abused. Five hundred individuals may be direct victims of sexual abuse in a small community of two thousand. If you attend a family reunion of one hundred close relatives, twenty-five could be sexual abuse victims."[5]

You and I must reach out to these women who suffer from the pain of childhood sexual abuse. We must reach out with needed help. We must not be startled by the statistics. We must be educated about how to respond, how to help.

What Happens When a Girl Is Sexually Abused?

In *Daughters Without Dads*, Lois Mowday writes:

> Victims of sexual abuse may develop sexual problems that may be acted out in opposite ways: promiscuity or

asexuality. . . . Numerous problems may result from sexual abuse: eating disorders, low self-esteem, difficulty establishing and maintaining healthy relationships, trouble coping with stressful situations, inability to grow in maturity, and blocked spiritual growth.

Therapy can be beneficial, but a daughter and her abusing father seldom reach a healing in their damaged, twisted relationship. Sexual abuse is such a horrifying violation of the woman that it is almost impossible to erase the damage done. Forgiveness can happen, but it is usually communicated between the involved parties and God—not between daughter and abusing father.[6]

Other Forms of Child Abuse

Sexual abuse is not the only abuse children may suffer at the hands of parents or relatives. They may also endure physical abuse, emotional abuse, and parental neglect.

Not until 1871 did a group form in the United States that opposed child abuse. In 1866, when Mary Ellen Wilson was abused by her adoptive parents, the American Society for the Prevention of Cruelty to Animals intervened!

Child abuse can come in many forms:

- Physical abuse: Slapping, pushing, kicking, shoving and injuring in other non-accidental ways. Physical abuse can be mild or it can be deadly.
- Emotional abuse: Degrading, rejecting, and threatening a dependent youngster. It may be withholding love and affection or using hateful words that destroy self-confidence.
- Child neglect: The child's basic physical, emotional, or spiritual needs are not met or parental love is not provided.

The National Center on Child Abuse and Neglect estimates that "one million children are abused each year, resulting in two thousand deaths."[7]

A 1996 Gallup study revealed that 26 percent of teens say they have been hit or physically harmed by a parent or by another adult in the household in the past year.

Children are to be loved; cared for; and physically, mentally, emotionally, and spiritually nurtured. Children require adults to help them, advise them, and guide them into adulthood. A distressful childhood can overshadow and even ruin an entire lifetime.

A hurt child will often grow into an adult who has no sense of self-worth. Without this important sense of self-worth, a person may be emotionally maimed for life.

Liz has also been the victim of another type of child abuse—parental abandonment. Every child's unspoken fear is to be abandoned, either emotionally or physically, by a primary caregiver.

More and more women today are carrying the burdens of childhood trauma. These burdens are affecting their marriages, their parenting, their jobs. We are made aware daily of how immature, selfish, and/or addictive behavior (such as behavior caused primarily by alcohol, sex, pornography, gambling, or drugs) are tearing apart our nation's families and breaking the hearts of our children—children who will grow into adulthood with severe problems.

We call these families dysfunctional families. They usually cannot give adequate physical, emotional, and spiritual guidance to their children. Growing up in a dysfunctional family can cause a lifetime of sorrow, problems, and general grief. Most often, the children of these unhealthy families will produce unhealthy families of their own.

Hurting Women

Is healing of childhood wounds possible, even wounds caused by sexual, emotional, or physical abuse? Can adult victims of childhood trauma find wholeness for their broken hearts and crushed spirits? Listen to Liz.

> Yes, healing is possible. We can recover hope. God can heal open wounds that fester with anger and hate.
>
> When Jenny [her Christian counselor] reached out to me, she helped me to understand that I was not at fault in the abuse. Jenny prayed with me and helped me to understand that God could so fill my heart and mind with His love, His forgiveness, and His strength, that I could find healing in Him even in the midst of my greatest struggles.

Liz reached out to Jenny. Jenny reached out to Liz. And both Christian women reached out to the Lord. Liz received the healing she sought so eagerly.

What was the primary discovery Liz made about God's healing? Over a period of time, God revealed to Liz that she could forgive her father for his actions toward her. She discovered what every woman abused in childhood can discover: Complete forgiveness comes directly from God and is the major force in emotional healing. The Holy Spirit gives us the power to forgive those who have caused us pain—not to excuse them for their actions but to forgive them willingly. Forgiveness has the power to relieve us from the pain of memories, to provide us once again with strength and joy in our lives.

What exactly is forgiveness?

Lewis B. Smedes wrote: "Forgiveness is God's invention for coming to terms with a world in which . . . people are unfair to each other and hurt each other deeply."[8]

Perhaps my favorite definition of forgiveness is this one, by Dr. Ray Burwick:

> Bear the reality of the hurt, then choose to remember it against him (or her) no longer. The person who forgives faces completely the extent of hurt or wrong dealt to him. He doesn't rationalize for it or for the person who offended him. He doesn't block it out of his mind. He doesn't cover or mask it with alcohol, drugs, shock treatments, or a life-style of busy-ness. He sets the offender free from the wrong and wipes the slate clean.[9]

A clean slate. Only through the power of the Holy Spirit can an abused woman truly forgive those impossible to forgive and wipe the slate clean. You and I must show hurting women how, through the Holy Spirit, to wipe the slate clean and begin a new life.

Who Is the Hurting Woman?

So often we don't know her name. We only know that she is a woman with a dreadful secret, a secret that lives in her heart and mind every day. She is embarrassed about her secret pain. For years she has suffered with it. She is the woman who smiles on the outside and churns on the inside. She's your next door neighbor. She sits beside you during Wednesday night church supper. She's your mother, your daughter, your granddaughter, your best friend. And she's hurting. She needs a healing touch.

You and I must introduce her to the Healer. We must encourage her to reach out to Jesus in faith. Like the woman who touched Jesus' robe, she can find wholeness. She can speak the words the woman of many years ago may have spoken:

> To my surprise, His voice was gentle. "Daughter," He said to me. I looked up into His eyes. He called me "daughter," as if I actually belonged to Him, to His family. It had been a long time since anyone had so lovingly, so purely, called me "daughter."
>
> He continued. "Your faith has healed you. Go in peace and be freed from your suffering."
>
> Devastation, shame, humiliation. All of these were gone from my life. I trusted Jesus with my painful secret. I reached out to Him, and He reached back to me with the love, help, and healing I needed most.

(Some names have been changed to protect the privacy of those involved.)

---

[1] Andrew D. Lester, *When Children Suffer* (From a chapter written by: Ratliff, Virginia D. and Ratliff, Bill J. "Abused Children.") (Philadelphia, PA: The Westminster Press, 1987), 134.

[2] Alice Huskey, *Stolen Childhood: What You Need to Know about Sexual Abuse* (Downers Grove, IL: InterVarsity Press, 1990), 14.

[3] Ibid.

[4] Lester, 134.

[5] Huskey, 36.

[6] Alice Mowday, *Daughters Without Dads* (Nashville: Oliver Nelson, 1990), 24.

[7] Cheryl McCall, "The Cruelest Crime," *LIFE*, December 1984, 58.

[8] Lewis B. Smedes, *Forgive and Forget: Healing the Hurts We Don't Deserve* (New York: Harper & Row, Publishers, 1984), xi-xii.

[9] Ray Burwick, *The Menace Within: Hurt or Anger* (Homewood, AL: Ray Burwick), 93.

Questions for Reflection and Discussion

1. What does the woman in Mark 5:1–34 have in common with Liz and Alice? How did society in biblical days deal with the hurting woman? How does our society deal with women wounded by terrible secrets? How can we best educate our society and church members to learn about, understand, and reach out to those wounded by painful pasts and show them the way to healing and wholeness?

2. Think about the statement: "Sexual abuse happens in families of all social levels, regardless of income, community prominence, or church affiliation."

   Do you know of a case where sexual abuse happened in a respected family?

3. "Sexual abuse usually leaves its young victim wounded and suffering with a deep sense of shame, guilt, and worthlessness." Do you think this is true? If yes, why?

4. Read and discuss the following: "Sexual abuse is a form of bullying, only worse. A little girl cannot understand this terrible trauma caused by an adult she trusts. She doesn't have the maturity to grasp what is happening to her. She is at the complete mercy of someone older, bigger, smarter. An innocent little girl is no match for an adult abuser."

   How can we be sensitive to a victim of childhood abuse and how this may affect her image of God as "Father"?

5. Think about and discuss Alice Huskey's story. In your opinion, did her mother react properly? What would you have done in this case? Do you believe that Alice suffered more from the abuse or from the disclosure of her secret? Alice Huskey writes: "I felt as if I had a big sign around my neck saying 'dirty, ugly, naughty, guilty—stay away.'" Do you believe this is a common feeling among victims of childhood sexual abuse? Why or why not?

6. Lois Mowday writes: "Victims of sexual abuse may develop sexual problems that may be acted out in opposite ways: promiscuity or asexuality. . . . Numerous problems may result

from sexual abuse: eating disorders, low self-esteem, difficulty establishing and maintaining healthy relationships, trouble coping with stressful situations, inability to grow in maturity, and blocked spiritual growth."

How do these problems discourage you in your attempts to reach out to victims of sexual abuse? Do you think you and I can learn to see through to the source of these problems and sincerely reach out with love and help?

7. Investigate support groups in your community who reach out to women who suffer from childhood sexual abuse. Make those phone numbers and addresses available to your church staff, especially those who work in women's ministry. If possible, start a support group in your own church. Bring together women who have been abused and have found healing with women who are still in their struggle to find healing and wholeness.

8. Sexual abuse is only one form of child abuse. Seek more information about child abuse and what you and your church can do about it. If you suspect child abuse occurring in your church or community, talk to your pastor or a trusted member of your church staff. Investigate the situation. If you discover that a child is being abused, work to stop it. *Precious in His Sight* by Diana Garland deals with this issue and many others. To order your copy, call WMU Customer Service at 1-800-968-7301.

Prayer

To close your personal devotional time or your group time, you may want to use the following prayer:

Father, show us how to reach out with needed help to women who have been hurt in childhood by abuse. Bring to those women Your healing, Your peace, Your blessing. Help them to forgive those who have hurt them so that they may find freedom and wholeness.

Alert us to children currently facing abuse. Teach us how to recognize abuse and how to stop it. We know that You love all Your children. Let us be Your heart so that we may love them too. Let us be Your hands so that we can reach out and offer them needed help. In the name of Jesus, the Healer, we pray. Amen.

Chapter 6: God's Heart, God's Hands

I Love You All, and I'm So Sorry: Reaching Out with Love

Helping Mothers of Suicide Victims

Bible Study: Read Luke 7:11–16

When death claims the person that a woman loves, she will go through a period of deep mourning. This time in life can be difficult, if not devastating. Overnight the loss of a loved one can dramatically change her life. She needs someone at that time to reach out to her with love.

Grieving women have said that the death of a child is the most difficult for them to bear. One woman described that when her healthy child died from a car accident, she grieved primarily because of the lost potential that child's untimely death represented.

Throughout history, mothers have had to deal with the untimely deaths of their children. The first mother, Eve, lost a son to untimely death. Women have lost children through disease, accident, murder, and suicide.

Let's consider the poor widow who lived in Nain at the time of Jesus. She already had lost her husband to death. We aren't told how her only son died, but she stood by his coffin and painfully mourned his untimely death. Perhaps he died of a disease untreatable in that day. Perhaps he died from an accident. We aren't told how he died. No doubt, this son provided the livelihood for himself and his mother.

When Jesus walked into Nain that day, He saw the grieving mother standing beside her son's dead body during the funeral. The emotional sight moved Jesus. It stirred His heart. Luke tells us that "when the Lord saw her, his heart went out to her" (Luke 7:13).

Jesus stopped and put His hand on the coffin, a definite taboo among the religious people of His day. No person of God was allowed to touch the dead for the dead were proclaimed unclean. Jesus reached out to the corpse. To the shock of the crowd, Jesus spoke to the dead man, "Young man, I say to you, get up!" (v. 14).

Scripture paints the unforgettable portrait: "Jesus gave him back to his mother!" (v. 15). In this mother's greatest time of need, Jesus reached out to her with love, with compassion, and with the gift of life resurrected from a still body.

Unlike Jesus, you and I cannot give a child back to a grieving mother. But we can reach out to her in the way Jesus often reached out to those who grieved the loss of a loved one. With love and compassion, we can give her Jesus' hope. We can tell her that Jesus not only reached out in love to a nameless widow at Nain, but He is alive today, and He can reach out to her in her deepest pain.

Only a short while after Jesus journeyed to Nain, He journeyed to Calvary. While the widow at Nain rejoiced in the company of her resurrected son, Jesus' mother stood and grieved beside Jesus' dead body. To the amazement of His mother and friends, however, three days later Jesus came back to life! Jesus' resurrection from the dead gives us hope of eternal life in Him.

Grief that Almost Never Ends

When a mother loses a child to death, she also loses that child's future. She carries that child with her all her life. The mother might think, "He would be a senior in high school, planning to enter college next year." "What would she look like as an adult?" The child is always growing up; the mourning never really ends.

Her son is the little one she nursed as a baby. With tears in her eyes, she sent him off to first grade toting his new book bag.

He is the one for whom she stood and cheered at his Saturday morning soccer games.

Her daughter is the little one she held all night waiting for the fever to break. This is the child she shopped with for her first white Easter shoes. When she played her first piano recital piece, this loving mother proudly clapped and told the mother seated beside her: "That's my daughter!"

A mother is devastated when an accident takes the life of her child. She sits by the hospital bed and prays for the child who is dying from disease. She experiences shock and intense anger when someone without conscience purposely takes the life of her child. But as difficult as these deaths are to accept, they aren't the most difficult. There is one kind of death that is so needless, so untimely, so horrifying that words fail to describe a parent's grief. That devastating death is suicide by a child's own hand.

A Child's Death by Suicide

Memories that used to bring such beautiful thoughts instead will be agents of pain and confusion when a child commits suicide. The question "why?" will be a constant companion. "The grief after suicide is one of the most difficult griefs persons ever experience. And the grief almost never ends, although its intensity diminishes," Bill Blackburn writes in his book *What You Should Know About Suicide*.[1]

Suicide used to be only whispered about when the victim's family wasn't in sight. Our society has opened up to the pain and problem of suicide. Suicide prevention and care for families experiencing suicide is coming to the forefront of our society.

Never has the epidemic of suicide become more prevalent among our nation's young people. Youth suicide now takes second place as the major cause of death among our young people.[2]

In this chapter we will directly confront the problem of suicide among our youth. We need to learn how to reach out to the woman who has been hurt by the suicidal death of her child. We also need to learn about warning signs and how they can lead to suicide prevention. Both prevention and care for those affected are essential to reaching out to women who experience this firsthand.

Elizabeth's Story

Elizabeth, 15, left prayer meeting early at her church and walked with a friend to her nearby home. On the way, Elizabeth told her friend she was going to finish cleaning her room and then kill herself. Thinking Elizabeth was being overly dramatic, her friend didn't take the threat seriously.

At 8:15, Elizabeth's mother found her in her room, dead from a self-inflicted gunshot wound.

The youth at church later told the parents that Elizabeth had talked often about killing herself, but subtly and almost jokingly. As early as six years before, Elizabeth had told a friend about finding a gun hidden in her parent's closet.

"We didn't tell any of our five children that we owned a gun," said Carolyn, Elizabeth's mother. "We kept it trigger-locked, unloaded, and hidden in the closet, with the trigger-lock key in another part of the closet."

Elizabeth went to a lot of trouble to find the gun, bullets, and trigger-lock key.

Elizabeth Hudson was a pretty girl who was dedicated to the Lord, active in church, successful in school, and musically talented. But Elizabeth had severe physical problems caused by congenital birth defects. She also had undergone major surgery several years before and suffered from chronic back pain. Her physical pain and condition also caused emotional pain.

"It is apparent to us now that Elizabeth had planned her death for some time," said Carolyn. "She made elaborate preparation in her room that Wednesday night. She placed her music awards neatly in a plastic laundry basket, turned photos of herself facedown, laid out clothes for her burial, and left a note."

The note began: "I love you all, and I'm so sorry."

Groping for Answers

We must reach out to those mothers and fathers who have been devastated by the suicidal death of a child. This crisis will test their faith as no other crisis can. Victims admit they turn almost inside out groping for answers, for understanding. "What did we do wrong?" usually is the first question they ask. "How could we have prevented it?" most often is the second question.

We can begin ministering to grieving family members by telling them that the warning signs of suicide are often missed.

The signs can be so subtle that even trained counselors can miss them. We can assure the hurting mother that the suicide of a child can happen for many reasons. Most parents who asked "What did we do wrong?" have done nothing wrong in their parenting. They are not responsible for the death of their child. We all make mistakes in our parenting because we learn parenting *as* we parent. But few of us make mistakes that would lead a child to his or her suicidal death. We need to reach out to the parents with sensitivity to answer those haunting questions they painfully consider but often do not verbalize.

Going back to work, school, or church after the news of the suicide has spread is intensely difficult. The stigma of suicide is very real, even in our ever-accepting society. Suicide can adversely affect the family members' relationships with one another, friends, co-workers, neighbors, and fellow church members.

"I look into the eyes of my friends, family, neighbors, and fellow church members and wonder what they're thinking about me, about our family, about our parenting," one mother said. "People we have known for years have begun to avoid us, are careful not to make eye contact, and don't know what to say or do."

Youth Suicide

Youth suicide deserves our deep concern, for it is quickly becoming a national crisis in this country. In 1990, more than 4,500 teenagers in the United States committed suicide, one every two hours. Some believe the number is two to three times higher since suicide often is reported as accidental death. Most experts agree that many adolescent deaths recorded as traffic accidents are really suicides. Many more young people have attempted suicide, but failed. The rate of youth suicide has more than doubled in the last two decades. Suicide is now the second leading cause of death among persons 15 to 24 years of age. A 1996 Gallup study shows that teen suicide has gone from 2.7 per 100,000 cases in 1950 to 11.1 per 100,000 cases in 1990. The five biggest factors leading to suicide are drug abuse, not getting along with parents, peer stresses, problems of growing up, and alcohol abuse. Fifty-nine percent of teens say they know someone who has attempted suicide. Twenty-six percent know someone who has succeeded. Fifty-five percent say they have discussed the topic with friends. Thirty-seven percent say they have considered taking their own lives. It touches every community across the country. In our homes, our neighborhoods, and in our churches, untold numbers of moms and dads, brothers and sisters, grandparents, teachers, classmates, and church-mates are grieving the young people who have chosen death over life.

As Christian women, you and I can have an effective ministry to women grief-stricken by a child's suicide. Hurting women are everywhere, wondering where they can find relief from the whys and hows. Perhaps the first way we can reach out to them is to seek understanding of the problem of youth suicide.

The Causes

What causes a young person to end his or her life? The reasons are varied, but some contributing factors are:

- loneliness
- isolation
- intense frustration
- depression
- a feeling of worthlessness and/or failure
- drug and alcohol use
- lack of family attention and/or family stability
- grief caused by divorce of parents
- the loss of a close friend to suicide. This often leads to a "copycat" or "cluster" suicide. According to psychiatrist Faye Doss, once a friend or classmate has committed suicide, suicide becomes a more acceptable alternative. Youth will often romanticize death and deny its finality.

In Elizabeth's case, intense physical and emotional pain motivated her.

Sometimes a young person will feel great pressure to achieve and will fear a possible failure. The high-achieving adolescent, obsessed with grades and success, may feel keen frustration when he or she can't perform to perfection. Suicide may seem an attractive way out.

Youth in crisis often perceive their problems as inescapable. They may feel an utter loss of control. During these times, they often cannot think clearly, make decisions, sleep, eat, or work. Most suicide victims don't really want to die, but they can't see a future without pain.

No Community Untouched

Suicide touches every church, every community. Experts predict the problem will increase. You might know someone who has lost a child to suicide. You and I can reach out in love.

Adolescent suicide most often is not a spur-of-the-moment decision. It comes after long-term feelings of depression, confusion, helplessness, and hopelessness. Yearning for freedom from deep emotional pain can drive youth to seek relief. Too often in their quest for peace and rest, youth choose this permanent solution.

What can you and I do? We can watch for suicidal warning signs and share them with others. We can intervene when possible. Some warning signs are subtle; we may not even notice them. Other warning signs shout to be heard; but, even so, we may miss them.

Suicidal symptoms in young people may include:

- irregular patterns in eating and sleeping
- changes in behavior, such as a sudden cheerfulness after a time of depression
- withdrawal from family, friends, and social activities
- a preoccupation with death and dying
- an increase in alcohol and/or drug use
- decreased interest in personal appearance
- lack of interest in hobbies, work, school, or other usual activities
- talking about committing suicide
- giving away prized possessions and beginning to prepare for death

Experts believe as many as 80 percent of potential victims communicate their desire to die before they attempt suicide.[3] Almost always, a parent feels overwhelming guilt for not recognizing the signs before the suicide. But even experts sometimes miss the warning signs.

Before we allow parents to start blaming themselves, let us help them understand how difficult society makes it for a parent and for a young person these days. Life demands much from a parent. In the exhausting day-after-day task of parenting; with the increasingly difficult job of keeping the family fed and sheltered; by sheer time, energy, and work demands a mother or father cannot be totally attentive toward the child. This is especially true if they have more than one child in the family. Parenting is a tough job. Sometimes even when parents do their best, something happens.

Parents must also realize they are not their children's only influence. Our society makes it difficult to rear a child. Our children are shaped and influenced by a culture addicted to sex, money, drugs, alcohol, gambling, the occult, and violence. Murder, sex, and crime in general often are sensationalized.

Sometimes parents are alerted to suicidal warning signs, but often a parent can fail to understand the signals until after the suicide has happened. Only in looking back do the pieces of the puzzle seem to fit together and show a true picture of the situation.

A Loving, Caring Church

Friends and concerned church members can sometimes step in and rescue the child from suicide. Sometimes, however, they cannot. The death occurs. The ministry and love we show the parents and other family members can make a great difference in their lives.

Elizabeth's family decided they should actively work to prevent other suicides. Word spread throughout the church the Wednesday night after her death. The pastor called a special meeting for the congregation. Counselors from a local high school and the city's crisis center gathered at the church to speak and to counsel with the large group assembled there.

One high school counselor said about that night, "The mood was tense, somber, and serious. Some of the kids were hysterical and blamed themselves for Elizabeth's death."

The next night, the church offered a course in suicide prevention for the entire church family. A week later Elizabeth's parents talked with the youth, parents, and friends at church about her death.

If a family in your church has experienced the suicide of a child, talk with your pastor and/or church staff. Even though this is an intensely personal crisis they are facing, minister to the family as Christ's representatives.

A Message of Hope

Following is a letter Carolyn wrote several months after Elizabeth's death. Perhaps you can share this letter with a mother who grieves over the death of her child. It contains a message that holds many answers for those experiencing the pain of losing a child.

In those dark days immediately following Elizabeth's death, I felt as if my very soul had been ripped apart. I felt like an empty shell of my former self; one merely going through the motions of living. At times I could not feel God's presence, the God who had always been there for me. He seemed so silent and distant, and I was too devastated even to pray for myself.

Yet somehow, in the middle of all this hopelessness and total despair, I began to feel little moments of comfort. The incredible hurt and pain were still there, but I began to feel God's presence again, maybe only for a few fleeting minutes; but I knew He was there, holding me up and walking beside me. Often I would receive a phone call or a note in the mail from a friend who had been praying for our family. Then I would think back on how the burden of pain and grief had seemed miraculously lifted for a time.

This final thought probably has been the single most comforting thing said to me since Elizabeth's death.

As a Christian I always have believed that God has given us two supreme gifts—our lives and the life of His Son Jesus Christ which was sacrificed for us. I was obsessed with this thought: *Would God be angry at Elizabeth for throwing His gift back in His face? Would He forgive her for taking her own life?*

I verbalized this thought to a young man who was a close friend of Elizabeth's. In wisdom which far surpassed his 18 years, he replied: "Are you angry at Elizabeth for taking her own life?"

I replied, "No, of course not." I knew the physical burden she carried from numerous congenital birth defects, and I knew the additional emotional pain her physical condition created. I ached with her. The burdens she had borne had broken my heart. I could never be angry with her.

Then he asked: "Is your husband angry with her?"

I again replied, "No."

Then he said, "How much greater and more perfect is her Heavenly Father's love for her than the love of her earthly parents."

My question was answered.

----
[1]Bill Blackburn, *What You Should Know About Suicide* (Dallas: Word Publishing, 1990), 143.
[2]Ibid., 29.
[3]Ibid., 33.

Questions for Reflection and Discussion

1. Respond to the following statement. "A child's death is different and more difficult to bear than the death of other loved ones. It means the loss not only of a person, but of a future. . . . The child is always growing up; the mourning never really ends."

2. Read and discuss the following paragraphs:

   If you notice suicidal behavior in a friend's child, ask the child if she is thinking about suicide. Sometimes we think that if we don't talk about suicide, it will go away. It will not. Be direct and talk openly. Be willing to listen.

   When talking with a youth who may be contemplating suicide, avoid being judgmental and refrain from giving advice. Never dare him or her to do it. Avoid asking why the youth is threatening suicide, since this often encourages defensiveness. Don't be sworn to secrecy but seek support from trusted others—parents, pastor, family physician, school counselor, or psychologist. If a suicide and crisis center is in your area, talk to the parents and ask them to contact the center.

   If you suspect a person is thinking about suicide, don't wait. Take immediate action. Your sensitivity and quick response could save a life. Continue to pray for the person, and keep assuring him or her of God's unconditional love.

3. Some ways your church and community can reach out to hurting people who may be considering suicide are:
   • Organize youth suicide prevention programs and seminars. Some churches have planned churchwide evenings where parents, youth, and church workers can listen to trained Christian counselors talk about suicide prevention.
   • Contact organizations in your community, local high school counselors, or the American Association of Suicidology (4201 Connecticut Avenue, NW, Suite 310, Washington, DC 20008; [202] 237-2280). Ask them to advise you on how to establish a suicide intervention program in your church.
   • Provide a safe place where troubled youth can talk to trusted Christian counselors who can help them.
   • Involve church youth in meaningful programs and social activities. Provide youth with weekly programs of Bible study, active leadership roles in church and choir, and regular fun and meaningful activities. Show them they belong to a church who prays for them, loves them, supports them, cares about the pressures they face, and believes they are an essential part of the church community.

What are other things your church and/or community can do?

4. Read 1 Corinthians 13. Think about and discuss the following:
   • In what ways do we, as Christian women, practice these concepts of love when we reach out to women who need our help?
   • Reread 1 Corinthians 13:13: "And now these three remain: faith, hope and love. But the greatest of these is love." Discuss why Paul might have placed love in a higher category than faith and hope.
   • Look up a dictionary definition of *love*. How does this definition differ from the definition Paul gave in 1 Corinthians 13?

5. Read John 19:25–27. In these verses, John gives us a beautiful relational insight between Jesus, His mother, and His friend. What do these verses show us about the remarkable love of Jesus as He prepared to die? What words would you use to describe this kind of love? (Example: unselfish, devoted).

6. In light of the insights about love you have gained from the above questions, in what specific ways can you and I help to prevent our youth from killing themselves? How can we make a difference?

7. Name ways we as individuals can show our young people that we love them, that they are important to us, and that we want them to have a fulfilling future in the Lord.

8. What can you and I do individually to help the grieving mother of a youth who has committed suicide? Why is it important that we reach out to her? What are some specific ways we can reach out to her?

9. How can we as concerned Christians pray for our nation's youth and families? What are some positive steps we can take to reduce or eliminate some of the factors (such as availability of weapons, glorification of violence, loneliness, isolation, hopelessness, a sense of worthlessness and/or failure, lack of family stability) that contribute to youth suicide?

Prayer

To close your personal devotional time or your group time, you may want to use the following prayer:

Our Heavenly Father, show us how to reach out with love to women who have had to deal with a child's suicide. Please allow us to love them and to talk with them about their child's death.

Help us to be women with open arms and loving hearts. Help our church to be especially sensitive and compassionate with those who are hurting by the loss of a loved one. May we pull close together in troubled times. May we cry together and embrace one another in times of tragedy and confusion. When hearts have been hurt by grief and despair, please show us how to reach out to them. We ask that You would bring healing to their hurting hearts through our loving hearts and caring hands. In Jesus' name, the One who gave the ultimate and eternal gift of love, we pray. Amen.

Chapter 7: I Love You All, and I'm So Sorry

God's Mighty Love and Faithfulness: Reaching Out with Faithfulness

*Helping Women Cope with
Loss and Grief*

Bible Study: Read John 20:1–18

We know little from Scripture about Mary Magdalene. Luke 8:2 tells us she was a follower of Jesus "from whom seven demons had come out." With demon possession, evil took control. We can only imagine what torture she must have felt before meeting Jesus and how she might tell her story to us today:

> They tormented me night and day causing me to cry out for rest, for death, for anything that could deliver me from their torture. I could not escape the evil spirits.
>
> Torment plagued me every waking moment and caused me to threaten and terrorize those in the town I yearned to embrace. Evil spirits growled through my voice, and I blushed at their words. I could not control them, I could not run from them. Madness, insanity, and fierceness became my identity to those I loved most. I could not fight, for I truly believed that evil had won, and I was its eternal victim.[1]

Then a stranger walked into my life one day. He came to Magdala, the city where I lived. He reached out to me, and with rare authority, ordered the seven demons from me. In an instant, I became the loving woman I had once been. Transformation. I have learned that nothing is too difficult for God to do. I have felt God's presence. I have seen God's mighty love and faithfulness.

Jesus, You reached out to me. You released me from the agonizing grip and pain of evil. You have given me a new identity—Your identity. You have given me a new life, a life in You. Please allow me to reach back to You. I will give You all I have to give, my love, my loyalty. I promise never to leave Your side. I will follow You even to the ends of the earth.

Faithful Follower

Mary Magdalene followed Jesus faithfully throughout His ministry. She became a vital part of the small group of women who traveled with Jesus and ministered to Him and His disciples.

When Roman soldiers arrested Jesus and His followers fled with fear, Mary stayed with Him.

When they nailed Jesus to the wooden cross, and left Him to die, Mary knelt at His pierced feet.

When they placed Jesus' body within a rock-hewn tomb, Mary crept through predawn darkness to envelop Him with fragrant spices.

She followed Jesus to the ends of the earth, to the cross, to His death, to the grave.

Jesus rewarded Mary's devotion. He reached out to her. Jesus healed Mary, He saved her, He gave her new life. Jesus encouraged Mary, He taught her, He shared with her the secrets of God. Jesus gave her purpose and hope and restored her girlhood dreams. And, finally, Jesus chose Mary. From among all His followers, Jesus of Galilee chose Mary of Magdala to announce His greatest victory, His victory over evil, His resurrection from the grave.

Imagine her excitement upon finding the stone moved and the Lord alive!

"I have seen the Lord!" she shouted to the small band of bewildered disciples who still cowered in fear and deeply mourned the death of their leader.

"I have seen the Lord!" Mary continues to shout through Scripture to you, to me, to unknowing millions of women.

The Pain of Loss

How often, during the course of life's journey, do you and I confront the effects of evil face-to-face? Evil somehow changes us. It torments us night and day physically, emotionally, mentally, and spiritually. We encounter trials every day. We lose a spouse to death or a marriage to disaster. We lose a child to gangs, to cults, to drugs. We lose vitality and youth. We suffer as cancer, leukemia, or AIDS destroys the healthy bodies of those we love. Loss is an inevitable part of life.

"Do you see this woman?" Jesus asks us.

Someone you know, someone you love, someone in your church—someone is hurting at this moment with the agonizing pain of loss.

Reach out to her. She needs your faithful assurance, your faithful touch. She needs to know that God is near, even when she asks her difficult questions of faith.

"Why, Lord?" we hear the women around us ask. "Why do You allow such terrible losses in our lives? Your Word tells us You love us. Your Word tells us You are all powerful. If You love us, if You can protect us and those we love, then why don't You?"

"Why, Lord?" is the eternal question, one echoed down through the centuries, one we cannot seem to answer satisfactorily.

Sandy's Story

I will never forget the morning I took my daughter, Alyce, to her first day of kindergarten. That day Alyce and I met five-year-old Sandy and her grandmother. Alyce and Sandy had the same teacher. During the 20 minutes I stayed with Alyce, I noticed that little Sandy never smiled. With tears in her eyes, and away from Sandy's hearing range, her grandmother spoke in hushed tones to the kindergarten teacher. I knew something was wrong, but not until Alyce and Sandy became best friends did I learn the reason for the whispering and sadness.

A few months before school had started, Sandy, her baby sister, and her mother and father were driving home from vacation. In the middle of a busy intersection, a speeding car ran the red light and struck their car broadside. The mother and father were killed instantly. A nearby trucker witnessed the crash and sprang from his truck to rescue Sandy and her sister, both of whom by some miracle were not seriously hurt. He quickly pulled Sandy from the wreckage and placed her into the arms of concerned onlookers. Then he turned and ran toward the crying baby still strapped in her infant seat. But just as he approached the car door, the car burst into flames, leaving no hope of rescue.

The Mystery

Why does God permit such horrible things to happen to people? What good can come out of these sad and senseless deaths? "Why?" is a question that philosophers, theologians, Christians, and children have cried out to God in deepest pain. This question can so quickly turn people away from God.

Evil seems the victor. I look around at Christian friends and I see such unexplainable loss and hurt.

- Ellen still has nightmares about her childhood as the victim of an incestuous father.
- Carrie still suffers the guilt of a long-ago abortion.
- Peg, a retired minister's wife, has suffered a lifetime of devastating back pain since her car accident as a newlywed.
- Jan, a wife and mother of three small boys, was abandoned and left emotionally and financially hurting by an irresponsible husband.
- Cherrie, a young mother of two, has just learned she has terminal cancer and only a few months to live.
- Brenda confides she struggles day after day with an alcoholic and abusive husband who won't seek professional help.
- Linda, a 40-year-old woman, is trying to understand and cope with the trauma of a broken marriage and rearing teenage boys by herself.
- Cheryl experienced betrayal by her two best friends, friends with whom she shared her heart, friends for whom she would have readily given her own life.
- Pat, a 28-year-old, has just lost her young husband from an unexpected heart attack.
- Laura, a single young woman, was the victim of rape.

- Margie, a single mother, has just lost her job and has no money and no prospects for another job.
- Cindy, a young woman with a splintered spine, will spend the rest of her life confined to a wheelchair.
- Kelly is deeply hurt to discover her son's homosexual lifestyle.
- Adrian's only daughter has just been diagnosed HIV-positive.

Deep loss. These women are hurting. Many still are trying to understand, trying to cope, trying to figure out the whys of life. They are asking the difficult questions of God.

A Suffering World

The daily problems and crises women face today can stagger the imagination. Life is so fragile, and our love for those closest to us can run deep. What affects those we love—our spouse, children, parents, friends, fellow church members, neighbors—can cause us to suffer too. When we love another, we hurt when they hurt; we grieve when they grieve. As Christian women, our hearts ache with a world that suffers. How often do we bow our heads, weep, and pray for someone we may not know but with whom we share the pain of life, experience, and loss.

Jesus was there for Mary Magdalene when she faced the evil of seven demons who tormented her. Mary Magdalene was there for Jesus when He faced the cross and death. When each experienced unbelievable pain and most needed a loyal friend, the other was there to reach out with the deep bond of friendship and faithfulness.

Perhaps it is in friendship and faithfulness that you and I can reach out to women who have been hurt by the sting of loss, the devastation of evil, the confusion of tragedy.

Betty's Story

Betty's youngest son, Mark, was addicted to cocaine. One day he left home "his clothes wet from perspiration and the weather severely cold." The evil of drugs had stolen him from her. She never heard from him again.

Betty wrote:

As I look back now, I believe that deep in my heart I knew he would not come back, but I couldn't face that then. My whole being agonized over him. I knelt on the floor in my kitchen that first night he was gone and cried to the Lord. The next two weeks the trauma was so painful to my mind and emotions I toggled between coping and breaking. During this time the grief and trauma were very evident on my face. I called it the "death look."

Tormenting thoughts came during the following weeks. Days and weeks began to turn into months. Every time I felt I could not go any longer without hearing from Mark, I prayed, weeping with such intense fervency I would dream about him at night.

Two years passed. One night I received a call from the sheriff's department. Mark's remains had been found.

I went through the normal reactions of anger and denial. It was traumatic, much more than I had expected. I thought I had been through it all, but the finality hurt; and I tried to hold on to Mark as long as I could.

Asking "Why?"

Evil. Pain. Why does God allow them? The hurting women in this world will ask you and me this question when they confront devastating losses. Perhaps it will be their first question.

In his book, *Disappointment with God*, Philip Yancey asks: "Is God unfair? Why doesn't he consistently punish evil people and reward good people? Why do awful things happen to people good and bad, with no discernible pattern?"[2]

God does not cause spouses to be abused, teenagers to kill themselves, or loved ones to die in car crashes. God does not cause our sons and daughters to become addicted to drugs or to die horrible, unexplained deaths. But if God is in control of you and me, then it stands to reason that He permits these things to happen.

"Why?" is a difficult question with a variety of answers. Some answers are mind-boggling, some are soaked in theological mumbo-jumbo, some are truly not biblically based, and some are just plain preposterous.

Often I have wondered if God gets tired of our asking Him difficult questions of faith. Can we, the creation, question the Creator?

Elisabeth Elliot, a woman of strong faith in God, knows first-hand about suffering, evil, grieving, and about asking the difficult questions of faith. She has reached millions for Christ through retelling her story. Through her own tragedy, she has spent a lifetime faithfully reaching out to other hurting women.

Elisabeth and her young husband, Jim, were missionaries to the Auca Indians in Ecuador, South America. They had been married only a short time when Jim and four other missionaries were savagely murdered in the Amazon rain forest. They were killed by people to whom they had come to minister, teach, and help.

In 1958, Elisabeth, her daughter Valerie, and another missionary returned to Ecuador to live and work with the Auca Indians. Five years after her husband's death, Elisabeth returned to the scene where her husband was murdered. She and Valerie were guided to the shallow graves by the natives who had killed the missionaries, the natives who were now converted to Christianity and were her friends.

As they walked along the river, they stopped at the place where the crime took place. The natives responsible for the deaths described to her what had happened that day.

As you read the story of Elisabeth Elliot, you ask "Why?" Why would an all-powerful and all-loving God allow five missionaries to travel so great a distance to spread the gospel and then permit them to be savagely murdered?

There are many things God allows to happen that we cannot understand. Why? Because God is God—perfect in every way. We are human—far from perfection. Our faith in God rests on His nature, character, and Word; not what we think He should do or allow.

A True Faith

The only answer we can give women who come to us seeking answers is that God is God. Perhaps that is the only answer we need to find. That is the only truth we need to cling to in times of trauma, confusion, and loss. God loves us and allows us to love Him or hate Him; to trust Him or doubt Him; to seek Him or reject Him; and, yes, even to ask Him questions.

Perhaps realizing that we do not, and never will, understand is the greatest understanding we can have. We have something very difficult to do in this life, and we must tell other women to do it too. We must trust. We must do the almost impossible.

With faithfulness, we must trust the One we cannot touch and put our arms around to hold, yet the One we know holds our fragile lives and the whole universe.

With loyalty, we must trust the One who died a death we cannot fully comprehend but know has made us right with God and heirs to His family.

With devotion, we must trust the One we cannot audibly hear yet promises to speak to us if we will listen.

With allegiance, we must trust the One we cannot see yet lives within us and promises never to leave us. Trusting God to this extent is not easy.

It takes a tough faith to believe that God came to earth, died, and raised Himself from death. No wonder the birth, life, death, and resurrection of Jesus Christ are stumbling stones in the path of those who don't believe. They are not logical! We are told to believe scientific and technological impossibilities (such as the virgin birth, Christ's miracles, and the resurrection) in an age of advanced science and technology.

But with assured faithfulness we must reach out to hurting women and tell them about the One who reached out first to us. Christ's faithfulness led Him to a cross.

You and I must believe and share this fact: we don't, and probably never will, understand the whys and ways of God. Until God chooses to reveal His will to us, we can only search, ponder, pray, and continue to seek understanding.

In the meantime, God permits us to endure suffering for reasons we do not understand. Perhaps it is a gift to us that God allows us to share with Him a broken heart. Scripture tells us that the heart of God has been broken again and again. Perhaps only in our sufferings can God fully come in, pull us closer to Him, and help us understand our lives in Christ.

God's Mighty Love

The Bettys of this world are all around us. They are the women hurt by evil and loss—the very ones to whom God reaches out through our hearts, through our hands.

Can you imagine the pain Betty endured when she watched evil devastate her son's young body with drugs?

Can you imagine the agony of waiting two years without one word for him to come home?

Can you imagine receiving the call from the sheriff?

Christian women have reached out to Betty with love, faithfulness, and understanding. Betty has stayed close to her Savior during her long ordeal. Listen to her closing words:

> I talked with a friend last week who lost her youngest son three years ago. She said, "The third year is the worst. I feel like I will always grieve; it is part of my identity."
>
> My heart rejected that statement. I grieved for many years over my son. I fought for his life, and I grieved as I saw him being pulled away by drugs. I grieved when I saw him change from a sweet, lovable kid into a bleary-eyed stranger. I grieved when he dropped out of school and his teenage years were stolen from him. I grieved when he disappeared. I grieved when his remains were found. I grieved at his memorial.
>
> But grief is not part of my identity. When my need was the greatest, God gave me more of Himself. When I hurt the most, God revealed more of His presence. I became aware of what Jesus really did on the cross. Nothing is too difficult for God to do—in our hearts, minds, or emotions. He helped me lay aside the past—sins, failures, wounds, and grief. Peace over Mark has filled my heart. Thoughts of him no longer consume my days. I have felt God's presence with me. I have seen God's mighty love and faithfulness.

The "Forever Pain"

Do you know someone who is tormented by the "forever pain"—the pain that is buried so deeply we think we never will be delivered from it?

You and I have a message for the wounded women of this world who cope with the "forever pain." Let us reach out to them and tell them that evil need not win control in their lives. Let us tell them that the battle already has been fought on a cross at Calvary. Jesus has conquered the Evil One. Evil can no longer claim eternal victims.

Let us tell these women that God's mighty love and faithfulness can heal their pain and deliver them from their torment.

Nothing is too difficult for the Lord. Just as He reached out to Mary Magdalene, He can reach out to these women and bring healing. They can be freed from demons that claw at them, twist their thoughts, and destroy their beautiful memories.

Jesus Christ can give the woman, hurt by loss and evil, a new identity, a new life. For He is the One Who is faithful. Eternally faithful.

(The name Sandy has been used to protect the privacy of those involved.)

---

[1]See *Holman Bible Dictionary*, "Demon Possession." The behaviors described are typical of demon possession, although we have no proof from Scripture that Mary Magdalene suffered from any or all of these behaviors.
[2]Taken from the book *Disappointment with God* by Philip Yancey. Copyright ©1988 by Philip Yancey. Used by permission of Zondervan Publishing House.
[3]Ibid., 38.

Questions for Reflection and Discussion

1. What do you think Philip Yancey meant when he asked these questions: "Is God unfair? Why doesn't he consistently punish evil people and reward good people? Why do awful things happen to people good and bad, with no discernible pattern?"[3] Do we have to understand why Christians suffer?

2. Name and briefly review stories told in the Bible of people who stopped and asked faith-searching questions (i.e., Job, David, Solomon, Jeremiah, Hosea, John the Baptist, etc.). What did God reveal to them?

3. "Our faith in God rests on His nature, character, and Word; not what we think He should do or allow." What does this statement mean to you? If you are part of group study, discuss your answer with others.

4. Webster's describes *faithfulness* as: "steadfast in affection and allegiance." From your Christian perspective, what could you add to this definition?

5. Mary Magdalene is mentioned 14 times in the Scriptures. What does this say about her devotion, her faithfulness, her purpose? Read John 19:25. What does this verse tell us about her devotion to Jesus?

6. Name some ways you and I can reach out to a bereaved mother on a deceased child's birthday, anniversary of the death, holidays, and other painful times.

7. Name and discuss some physical reactions women experience after the loss of a child or spouse. (For example: gaining or losing weight, not sleeping or sleeping too much, or becoming ill.)

8. Name and discuss the emotional reactions women experience after the loss of a child or spouse. (For example: depression, anger, frustration.)

9. Name and discuss the spiritual reactions women experience after the loss of a child or spouse. (For example: questioning God's love and faithfulness, questioning God's power, questioning their own faith in God.)

10. Contact a woman who recently has experienced loss of health; loss of a spouse through death, divorce, or abandonment; or loss of a child. Reach out to her as a group. Investigate support groups for those dealing with devastating losses. Consider starting a grief support group in your church.

Prayer

To close your personal devotional time or your group time, you may want to use the following prayer.

O Lord, so often we don't understand why evil stalks our lives. We don't understand why our children become addicted to drugs, join violent gangs, or die senseless deaths. We are a world of people who are hurt by this evil, who cry in the still hours of the night, who ask the difficult questions of life and faith.

Be near us when we hurt. Carry us when we can no longer walk in such pain. Deliver us from our suffering and from those who would torment us. Let us look to You for healing and wholeness. Let us learn to depend on Your mighty love and faithfulness. Help us to reach out with love and loyalty to those around us who, at this moment, struggle, hurt, and are desperate to be freed from their pain. Help these women to find a new identity, a new hope, a new purpose in You.

Let us be Your heart, Lord. Let us be Your hands. Let us love as You would have us love. Amen.

Chapter 8: God's Mighty Love and Faithfulness

The Hope That Never Dies: Reaching Out with God's Eternal Hope

Helping Women Find Hope in Christ

Bible Study: Read John 4:4–42

A message to take to your own heart and a message to share with all those who hurt.

This morning, I awoke early and looked out the dining room window. It is autumn in Birmingham, Alabama, my favorite city, and my favorite time of year. The mountains around my home are covered with trees, and the trees sparkle with color. I blink my eyes to make sure that the glowing world of emerald, gold, and ruby around me is real. Clouds of mist have nestled into the mountain valleys beneath a sky that we might call gray, but that C. S. Lewis would call "silver, dove, and pearl."

Winter will be here soon. The leaves will wither, brown, and die. The freezing rains, sleet, and snow will bury us in their seeming grip of death.

But when winter comes, and all seems dark and cold and gloomy, we can be sure that spring is not far behind. We can look forward to the budding trees and blooming flowers that we know will burst forth into the warmth and beauty of summer. New life. Abundant life. That is our hope, and we can depend on it.

Isn't life somewhat like the seasons? Beneath the tragedies and sorrows of life, beneath thick facial masks that hide our pain, beneath the anxieties, hurts, and broken dreams, the seeds of hope live on. God has placed in each of us the vision of forever. God planted deep within our hearts the hope of home. And hope never dies.

New Hope

The last 30 years have been difficult for women. Divorce and spouse abandonment have torn apart the cords of marriage and commitment. Women and children are enduring physical, emotional, and mental abuse every day. A dark hopelessness shadows the hearts of our young people and leads them to suicide. As women's roles in society are changing so drastically, women are placing unrealistic expectations on themselves, expectations that drain them of time with God, of energy, family relationships, and personal creativity. Life is losing its sacredness in society as indicated by trends such as increased violence, suicides, and cases of euthanasia.

The last 30 years have brought about a sexual freedom that has resulted in severe loneliness. We are living in a "make me feel good now" generation with little thought about tomorrow, our children, our resources, or our planet. Sexually transmitted diseases are on the rampage. Children having children is now commonplace. Violence rules our streets and makes us imprison ourselves within the professional security systems of our homes. We fear for our children, for their safety, for their learning of values, for their education, for their spirituality. Sex and brutality march across the television screen unashamedly while young minds soak up the example and allow the media to influence their behavior.

You and I and other Christian women face problems today that our mothers and grandmothers never had to face. And these problems are hurting us, even destroying us.

A book is not nearly long enough to explore, or even touch upon, all the problems that Christian women face today. Within these pages, however, we have tried to deal with at least some of the trauma from which women suffer. I truly believe that Jesus expects us, as dedicated Christian women, to reach out to His children, these hurting women who need to know Him. They need to know that, in Christ, they can find recovery, new life, purpose, and hope.

God's Heart, God's Hands

May you and I become God's heart and God's hands. May we forever reach out to women the way Jesus Christ reached out to hurting women in His day. Jesus set the example you and I are to follow. Jesus shows us how to reach out with affirmation, love, faithfulness, needed help, God's truth, forgiveness, prayer, and compassion. You and I must introduce the hurting women of this world to Jesus, for He, and only He, is the Hope that never dies, God's eternal Hope.